I am a
HINDU

I am a
HINDU

Manju Aggarwal
meets
Gaytri Devi Goswami

Photography: Chris Fairclough

Religious Consultant: A. T. S. Ratna Singham

WATTS BOOKS
LONDON • NEW YORK • SYDNEY

Gaytri Devi Goswami is eleven years
old. She and her family are Hindu.
Her father, Giriraj Prasad Goswami,
is a Brahmin priest. Her mother,
Shanti Devi, works in a factory in
East London. Gaytri's sister Kunti is
thirteen years old. Her brother Prem
Raj is fourteen and Damoder, her
other brother, is sixteen. The family
came to Britain in 1980 from India.

Contents

© 1984 Watts Books
Paperback edition 1993
This edition 1995

Watts Books
96 Leonard Street
London
EC2A 4RH

Franklin Watts Australia
14 Mars Road
Lane Cove
NSW 2066

ISBN 0 86313 168 9 (hardback)
ISBN 0 7496 1406 4 (paperback)

Text Editor: Brenda Clarke
Design: Peter Benoist
Illustration: Tony Payne

Printed in Hong Kong

The Publishers would like to
thank the Goswami family
and all other people shown
in this book.

The Hindu belief

My family follow a religion called Hinduism which began in India thousands of years ago.

Hinduism is one of the oldest religions in the world. Its beginnings can be traced back to 2,500 BC in ancient India. The name Hindu was first used to describe the people who lived near the Indus River. The beliefs of these people became a religion and a way of life which spread throughout India.

We believe that God can be seen and worshipped in many ways. Our family worship the god Krishna.

All Hindus believe there is one supreme God called Brahman found everywhere in the world. Some believe that there are many gods who are parts of the supreme God. These gods look like humans or animals. Each has different powers. Hindus choose the ones they like best. Some Hindus use other symbols, such as a sacred flame, to worship God.

Worship at home

We have a prayer room in our home where we keep images of our gods. My father is a priest so we have many ceremonies to do.

Most Hindus have images or pictures of gods in their homes. Some homes, as here, have special rooms for worship. Gaytri's father is a Brahmin, a member of the Hindu priest class. He has chosen to spend all his time at home and worship his gods.

We begin the day by waking the gods and washing their images. My father puts tilak on his forehead.

The images of the gods are put in special small beds at night and on a platform during the day. There are different prayers to say and ceremonies to carry out with the gods throughout the day. Tilak is a religious symbol showing the particular belief of the wearer.

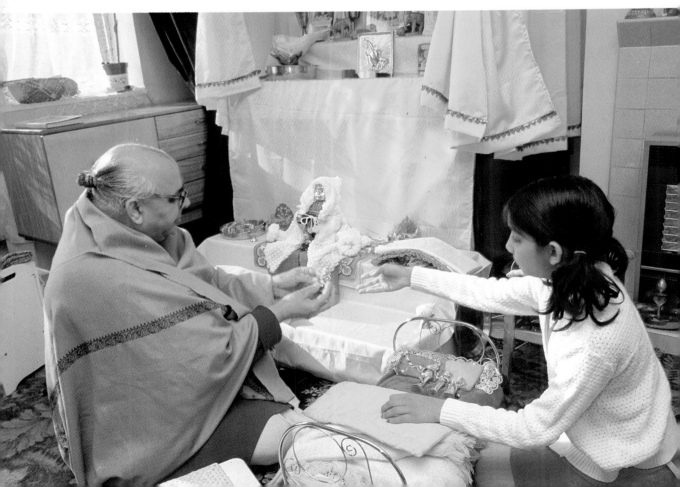

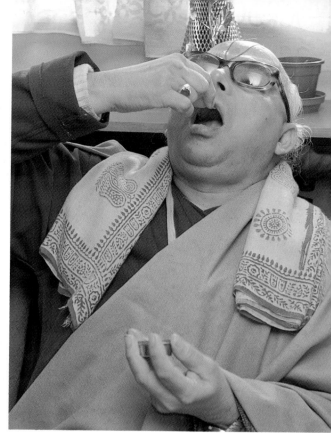

Daily worship and music

My father offers food to the gods in a special ceremony. He also prays and sings hymns.

The food offered to the gods becomes holy. When eaten by the worshipper it is called prasad. The person believes that the food has been shared with the gods. The same ceremony is done for all meals of the day. At night the gods are put back into their beds.

10

My father is a musician and a singer. I am learning to play the harmonium.

Most Hindus are very fond of music and it is used in many religious ceremonies. There are many different Indian musical instruments. Stringed instruments are more popular than wind instruments. The harmonium, shown in the picture, is like a small piano. Others are the sitar – a large stringed instrument like a guitar and the shennai, which is similar to the oboe.

11

Going to the Temple

We sometimes go to the temple to worship. Everybody has to take off their shoes to show respect.

As Hindus believe that God is everywhere, they can worship both at home or in a temple, called a mandir. For many the home is the main place of worship. Each temple has a main god, but there are always images of several other gods. Ganesh, the elephant-headed god, is the main god in the temple shown here. Prayers are said in front of a sacred flame.

I like the ceremony of Arti which the priest does in the temple.

The priest holds a tray with five candles and moves it slowly in front of a god. Then the tray is brought around to everybody in the temple. The people hold their hands over the candles then they pass their hands over their forehead and hair. Offerings of money are made and the holy food prasad is eaten. During Arti hymns are sung to show love and devotion to God. The sacred word 'OM' (above right) is chanted.

The Hindu gods

There are many beautiful statues of our gods in the temple. We respect them all although our family god is Krishna.

Each god is said to be a different part of the supreme God. A Hindu has to choose which one to worship. Vishnu is thought to be gentle and kind. He has many different human and animal forms. One of these is Krishna (below left), who appeared on earth to save mankind.

Shiva (left, in the circle) is thought to be a fierce god who rules life and death. Shiva also has many different forms. Some of these are goddesses such as Kali and Durga (above left) who have great power. Ganesh (above right), the elephant-headed god, is prayed to when starting something, like moving into a new house. Hindus also believe that things in nature are forms of God. The River Ganges in India is said to be holy. Pilgrims go to bathe in the river and wash away their sins.

15

The Holy Books

My father reads the Holy Books to us every day. I am also learning Sanskrit.

Hinduism has several Holy Books. The oldest are called the Vedas. These are collections of hymns which tell about the nature of the world and how to worship gods. For thousands of years they were not written down but learnt by memory by all children of the Brahmin (priest) class. They were then written down in Sanskrit.

The Hindi Script

A अ	Ā आ	I इ	Ī ई	U उ
Ū ऊ	ṚI ऋ	ṜI ॠ	LṚI लृ	
É ए	AI ऐ	O ओ	AU औ	(M) अं
Ḥ अः	K क	KH ख	G ग	GH घ
Ṅ ङ	C च	CH छ	J ज	JH झ
Ñ ञ	Ṭ ट	ṬH ठ	Ḍ ड	ḌH ढ
Ṇ ण	T त	TH थ	D द	DH ध
N न	P प	PH फ	B ब	BH भ
M म	Y य	R र	L ल	V(W) व
SH श	Ṣ ष	S स	H ह	KSH क्ष
TR त्र	JÑ(GÑ) ज्ञ			

When I am older I will read the Upanishads. They are too difficult for me at present.

The Upanishads explain the place of man in the universe. They say that a person can be born again after death. One's actions in this life will affect what form, human or animal, one will be re-born into. After a perfect life one will be freed from birth and death to join God. Later writings such as the Bhagavad Gita describe the various duties of man.

The history of Gaytri's family

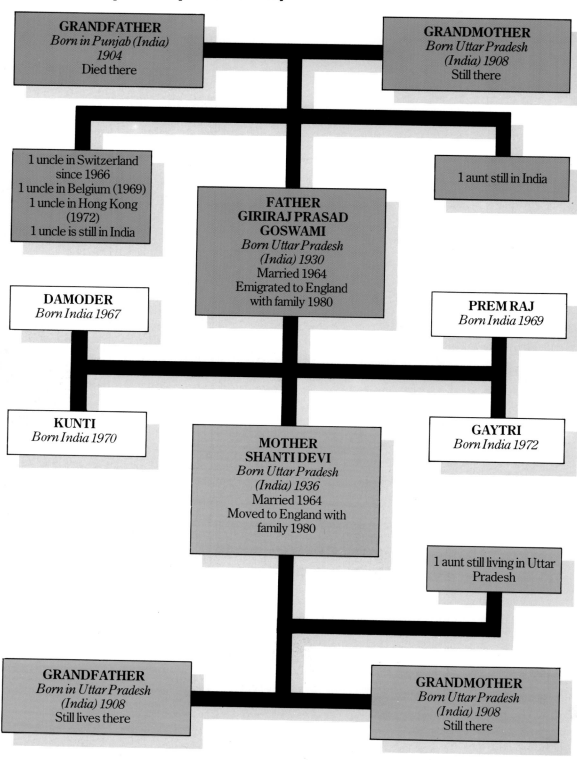

GRANDFATHER
Born in Punjab (India)
1904
Died there

GRANDMOTHER
Born Uttar Pradesh
(India) 1908
Still there

1 uncle in Switzerland
since 1966
1 uncle in Belgium (1969)
1 uncle in Hong Kong
(1972)
1 uncle is still in India

FATHER
GIRIRAJ PRASAD
GOSWAMI
Born Uttar Pradesh
(India) 1930
Married 1964
Emigrated to England
with family 1980

1 aunt still in India

DAMODER
Born India 1967

PREM RAJ
Born India 1969

KUNTI
Born India 1970

GAYTRI
Born India 1972

MOTHER
SHANTI DEVI
Born Uttar Pradesh
(India) 1936
Married 1964
Moved to England with
family 1980

1 aunt still living in Uttar
Pradesh

GRANDFATHER
Born in Uttar Pradesh
(India) 1908
Still lives there

GRANDMOTHER
Born Uttar Pradesh
(India) 1908
Still there

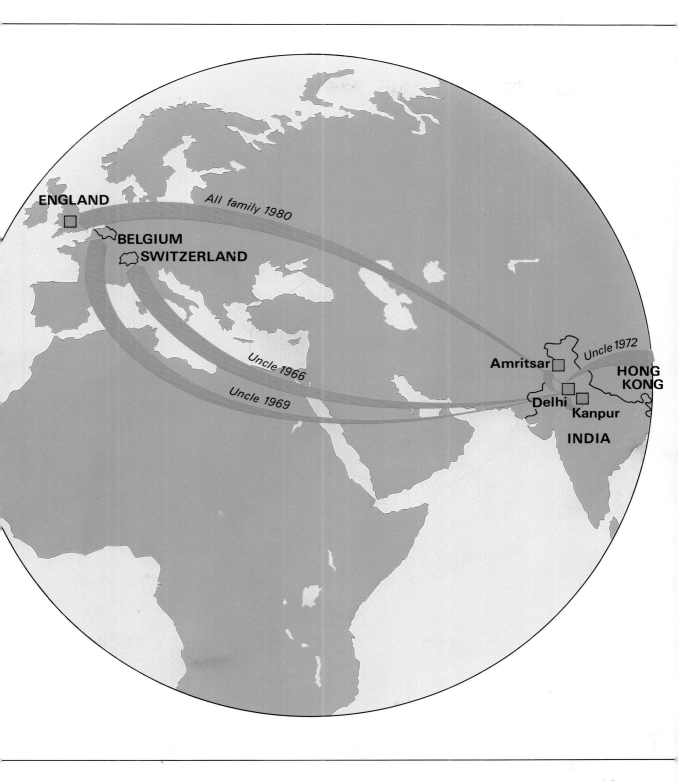

ENGLAND

BELGIUM

SWITZERLAND

All family 1980

Uncle 1966

Uncle 1969

Uncle 1972

Amritsar

Delhi

Kanpur

HONG KONG

INDIA

What a Hindu wears

My mother and father wear the same type of clothes they wore in India. I only wear a sari on special occasions.

There are no special Hindu clothes. A person wears the clothes of the family birthplace or what is best for the country in which they live. In Britain most men wear western clothes. Most women still prefer to wear the traditional Indian dress — the sari.

My mother has taught me how to put on a sari in the proper way.

A sari is made from one piece of cloth which is between 110 cm and 140 cm wide and 5 m to 8 m long. The cloth is wrapped around the waist and tucked into a petticoat to form a skirt. The rest of the cloth is put over the top of the body and shoulder in different styles according to the family birthplace in India. Many Indian women wear a jewel in their nose and many bracelets.

Eating the Hindu way

My family does not eat meat. We go to shops where they sell special Indian vegetables, herbs and spices.

Most Hindus from Northern India are vegetarians as it is thought wrong to kill animals. Hinduism teaches respect for all forms of life. Some Hindus do eat meat but not beef. The cow is a holy animal to Hindus. Vegetables are prepared in many different ways. Many herbs and spices are used to give flavour.

My mother still cooks the same kind of food we had in India. I like the curries, but not too hot!

Each part of India has its own special cooking. The meal shown here includes puri – a type of bread fried in butter, matar-panir – a vegetable curry with peas and curd cheese, rice and pédā – made out of milk, sugar and nuts. Hindus have many rules about how to eat. Cleanliness is very important and some will only eat with people of their own class.

Customs and festivals

We have many celebrations and festivals each year. I look forward to them very much.

Hindu festivals are happy occasions. The first event in a Hindu's life is the name-giving ceremony. This has to take place before the first birthday. The child is fed its first spoon of rice. A major festival each year is Diwali, in honour of Rama. Homes are lit by lamps, candles and even sparklers. Firework displays are also held.

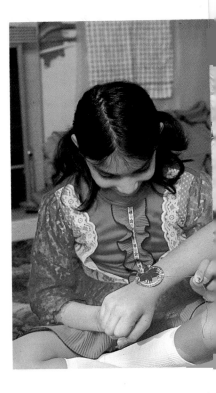

One of my favourite festivals is Holi when we throw coloured powder and water at each other.

Many Hindu festivals celebrate the start of a season of the year. Holi is the start of spring. It also remembers the gods Radha and Krishna who were happy lovers. Navaratri, a nine-day festival in the autumn, is dedicated to Durga and celebrates motherhood. Raksha Bandhan is the festival of protection. Girls tie a symbol called a rakhi on a brother's wrist in return for his protection.

The Hindu year

Hindus use the lunar calendar which means that the months start with each new moon. The first month of the year is Vaisakha and New Year's day is in the first or second week of April.

DEEPAVALI
(DIWALI)
Karttika – 5 days of which the 3rd day is the most important
Means 'the row of lights'. At this time Rama returned to his kingdom after a 14 year banishment. Commonly known as the Festival of Light.

VIJAYA DASHAMI
(DASHEHRA)
Asvina – 1 day
Celebrates the triumph of Good over Evil. On this day Rama defeated the ten-headed Ravana.

NAVARATRI
Asvina – 9 days
Festival devoted to Durga, the symbol of motherhood.

GANESH CHATURTHI
Bhadrapada – 1 day
Festival of Ganesh, the God of Good Omen with the elephant head. Particularly celebrated in Maharashtra.

ONAM
Bhadrapada – 1 day
Harvest festival. The most important festival in Kerala.

RAKSHA BANDHAN
Shravan – 1 day
Festival of protection which celebrates Indra, the king of the heavens, being protected by a rakhi when fighting demons. On this day girls tie a rakhi on a brother's wrist in return for his protection.

JANMA ASHTAMI
Shravan – 1 day
The birthday of Krishna, Vishnu's reincarnation. Celebrated all over India, especially in Krishna's childhood homes.

RATH YATRA
Ashadha – 1 day
The festival is held in Puri in Orissa in honour of Lord Jagannath (Lord of the Universe).

DECEMBER MARGASIRSHA NOVEMBER KARTTIKA OCTOBER ASVINA SEPTEMBER BHADRAPADA AUGUST SHRAVAN ASHADHA JULY

Around the outer rim (calendar wheel): JANUARY · PAUSA · MAGHA · FEBRUARY · PHALGUNA · MARCH · CHAITRA · APRIL · VAISAKHA · MAY · JYESTHA · JUNE

BIRTHDAY OF SWAMI VIVEKANANDA
Pausa – 1 day
Founder of Aryasmaj, a branch of Hinduism. His birthday is celebrated all over India.

SARASWATI PUJA
Magha – 1 day
Celebration in honour of Saraswati, the Goddess of Knowledge.

PONGAL
(SANKRANTI)
Magha – 3 days
Harvest festival. In Southern India the sun is worshipped on the first day, and elsewhere cattle are honoured.

HOLI
Phalguna – 1 day
Celebrates Spring. A happy festival when people often throw coloured powder and water over each other.

SHIVARATRI
Phalguna – 1 day
For all Hindus a solemn festival devoted to the worship of Shiva.

UGADI
(NEW YEAR)
Chaitra – 1 day
The Hindu New Year according to the lunar calendar.

PURAM
Vaisakha – 1 day
In Kerala in India there is an impressive festival at the temple of Shiva. It ends with firework displays.

RAM NAVAMI
Vaisakha – 1 day
The birthday of Rama, held on the 9th day of the month. It is a day of fasting and readings are made from the Ramayana.

VAISAKHI
Vaisakha – 1 day
This is the beginning of the solar New Year and is observed all over the UK. The River Ganges is believed to have been created on this day.

29

Hindu facts and figures

Hinduism is the third largest religion in the world with about 550 million followers. The largest is Christianity with about 1,000 million and then Islam with about 600 million followers.

The great majority of Hindus live in India where over 80% of the population follow the religion. In Pakistan only 11% are Hindus. Hindus are found in many other parts of the world. East Africa has the largest number in one area outside India and Pakistan. There are also communities in Sri Lanka, Nepal, Bali in Indonesia, Europe, Canada and the USA.

In Britain there are about 300,000 Hindus. Most of these came to Britain from East Africa and the rest mainly from India and Pakistan.

Hinduism is the world's oldest major religion. It can be traced back to at least 2,500 BC in the Indus Valley in India. The oldest Holy Book, the Rig Veda, was compiled by about 1,000 BC. The Holy Books include the four Vedas – Rig, Sama, Yajur and Atharvan, the Upanishads, the Ramayana and the Mahabharata which includes a famous section called the Bhagavad Gita.

The main Hindu beliefs include:

The unity of all things in the world. The spirit of God, Brahman, is said to run through everything in the world – plants, animals and humans.

Ahimsa – the belief that it is wrong to hurt any living thing.

Samsara – the cycle of life and death. One is re-born into another form after death until the highest state, called Moksha, is achieved through a perfect life.

Karma – a person's behaviour and actions in this life will decide their next life.

Dharma – a person has certain duties to family, class and to God.

Hinduism divides humans into social groups or castes. People are born into their caste. The four main classes of caste, in order of importance, are Brahmins – priests, Kshatriyas – warriors and rulers, Vaishyas – merchants and farmers and Shudras – peasants and labourers. A further class called Untouchables did all the very unpleasant work. Today the strict divisions of the caste system are being ignored by many Hindus.

Glossary

Bhagavad Gita A Holy Book also known as 'The Song of God'. It is a long poem in which God takes the form of Krishna.

Brahman The Hindu word for God. The origin and essence of the universe.

Brahmin The priest class of Hindu society.

Dowry Money or goods given by the bride's father to the bridegroom on marriage.

Ganges The holy river of India.

Ganesh The elephant-headed god who is prayed to for success in new ventures and business.

Gaytri A holy hymn to the sun found in one of the Vedas.

Hindu A person who follows the Hindu religion. It was first used by ancient Persians to describe the people living by the river Indus in the Punjab in India.

Krishna A god who appeared on earth to save mankind – known also as the god of love.

Mandir A Hindu temple.

Moksha Freedom from the cycle of life and death and unity with God.

Prasad Holy food shared with the gods during worship.

Sanskrit The ancient language in which the Hindu Holy Books are written.

Sari The traditional dress of Indian women made from one piece of cloth.

Shiva The god who rules life and death. The destroyer and creator of all things in the world.

Vedas Four Holy Books which are the oldest written statements on Hindu belief. The Rig Veda was compiled about 1,000 BC.

Vegetarian A person who does not eat meat.

Upanishads Holy Books which contain many of the most important statements of the Hindu religion. Compiled about 500 BC.

Vishnu A kind and gentle god who aids mankind to escape the forces of evil.

Index

T H E B O O K O F

SOUPS

LORNA RHODES

Photographed by
JON STEWART

TED SMART

Specially produced for Ted Smart,
Guardian House, Borough Road, Godalming, Surrey GU7 2AE.

This book was created by Merehurst Limited
Ferry House, 51/57 Lacy Road, Putney, London SW15 1PR.

ISBN 1 85613 105 X

Commissioned and directed by Merehurst Limited
Managing Editor: Felicity Jackson
Editor: Beverly LeBlanc
Designer: Roger Daniels
Home Economist: Lorna Rhodes, assisted by Linda Tubby
Photographer: Jon Stewart, assisted by Kay Small
Typeset by: Angel Graphics
Colour separation by: Kentscan Limited
Printed in Belgium by Proost International Book Production

ACKNOWLEDGEMENTS

The Publishers would like to thank the following
for their help and advice:
David Mellor, 26 James Street, Covent Garden, London
WC2E 8PA, 4 Sloane Square, London SW1W 8EE
and 66 King Street, Manchester M2 4NP.
Elizabeth David Limited, 46 Bourne Street, London SW1
and at Covent Garden Kitchen Supplies, 3 North Row,
The Market, London WC2.
Philips Domestic Appliances, 420-430 City House,
London Road, Croydon CR3 3QR.

Notes:
All spoon measurements are equal.
1 teaspoon = 5 ml spoon.
1 tablespoon = 15 ml spoon.

CONTENTS

INTRODUCTION

Soups are the most versatile and varied dish on a menu. One is spoilt for choice given a soup can be made from every type of food – fruit, vegetables, meat, poultry, fish or game. Soups can be uncooked and cold, to provide a refreshing opening to a summer meal, or hot and satisfying to make a warming start to a winter meal. A soup can be served as an elegant starter, become a snack served in a mug with crusty bread, or it may be so chunky and thick it becomes a whole meal in itself.

The choice of ingredients can be exotic and unusual, and may be expensive like lobster for a special occasion; but choosing cheap ingredients such as root vegetables or dried beans can result in an equally delicious soup. The combinations of textures, flavours and colours are endless.

There are over 100 exciting soup recipes in this book ranging from traditional British favourites to those from the cuisines of France, Italy, Germany, Spain, Russia, the United States, Australia and the Far and Middle East. Each is illustrated in colour and has step-by-step instructions for making the soup, plus many appealing ideas for garnishes and accompaniments.

SOUPS

Soups are ideal for every occasion, and the recipes in this book show just how varied and interesting they can be. Within each chapter there are clear soups, simple puréed soups, soups thickened and enriched with cream and eggs, some flavoured with herbs and others with spices. Making soups yourself means that they are nutritious and free from additives, preservatives and colourings. The flavour and texture can be adjusted to suit individual tastes.

The basis of most soups is a well-made stock. This is made by simmering meat or bones, a chicken carcass or fish heads and bones with aromatic vegetables and herbs, or just vegetables and herbs, to give a well-flavoured liquid. Stock needs to be simmered for a long time, and to be realistic we may not always have the time to make it. If you do, however, it is worthwhile making a large quantity and freezing some. There are excellent stock cubes available, and in many recipes they can be adequately substituted. If they are too salty, use less of the cube than recommended on the packet.

Consommé

It is essential to have a good home-made stock to make consommé – this is a clear soup made from enriched stock which is then clarified to give a crystal clear liquid. The consommé can be garnished with a wide variety of ingredients which are always dainty and carefully prepared. Consommé makes an elegant start to any meal.

Broth is also made from stock but it is not clarified, and the meat or chicken used to make the broth is often served in the soup.

Seasoning

An important rule in soup making is to season towards the end of cooking. Often a liquid reduces during simmering and the flavours of the ingredients mature so that the soup becomes more concentrated in flavour. Taste at the end, then season. Pepper should always be ground into the soup at the last moment to capture its full aromatic and spicy flavour.

Chilled soups should always be tasted after the chilling period and may need extra seasoning.

Thickening

There are various ways a soup can be thickened – simply puréeing the ingredients in a blender or food processor reduces the mixture to a smooth consistency – but try varying the texture by not always blending the soup until completely smooth.

Alternatively, in some recipes further sieving of the soup may be recommended after puréeing, to discard pips and skins of vegetables or bones from fish.

Using cream and eggs beaten together is called a liason and will enrich a soup and act as a thickener. Always remember to add a little hot soup to the liason before whisking it into the soup to prevent curdling.

Freezing

Sometimes it is difficult to make a small quantity of soup. If you have extra, cool the surplus quickly and then freeze it. Most soups freeze well and it is an excellent way of using up gluts of vegetables or tomatoes.

Avoid adding garlic to a soup which is to be frozen. Also, cream, eggs or milk should not be included before freezing, as these can cause curdling; add them at re-heating stage.

Use delicate fish soups and oriental soups immediately after preparation or the flavour and texture will deteriorate and re-heating will spoil the soup. On the other hand, the robust meat soups, like oxtail, benefit from being refrigerated overnight as the flavours mature and mellow.

Garnishes

A wide range of garnishes can be used to add extra interest to soups, from the simple sprinkling of fresh herbs, grated cheese or swirls of cream, to croûtons which can be made in lots of ways with a wide variety of flavourings. Rice and pasta can be used not only as a garnish but also to make some soups more substantial, as can dumplings which come in an assortment of flavours. The recipes in this book include simple garnishes of cooked and raw vegetables, such as onion rings, diced peppers or cucumber slices, as well as more involved accompaniments, such as choux puffs and cheese-filled pastries.

CHILLED FISH SOUP

500 g (1 lb) unpeeled cooked prawns
2 strips lemon peel
2 bay leaves
2 blades mace
salt and pepper
4 small squid, cleaned and gutted
2 spring onions, green parts only, chopped
4 tomatoes, skinned, seeded and chopped
2 tablespoons peeled and chopped cucumber

Peel prawns, putting shells, heads and tails into a saucepan. Reserve prawns. Cover with 940 ml (1½ pints/3¾ cups) water and add lemon peel, bay leaves, mace and salt and pepper.

Bring to the boil, then cover and simmer for 30 minutes. Strain stock through a muslin-lined sieve or coffee filter paper. Return stock to rinsed-out pan. Cut squid into thin rings and chop tentacles. Add to pan and cook for 5 minutes. Set aside to cool.

Stir in spring onions, tomatoes, cucumber and reserved prawns. Season if necessary. Chill for at least 1 hour before serving.

Serves 4.

SUMMER AVOCADO SOUP

2 ripe avocados
3 teaspoons lemon juice
1 clove garlic, crushed
155 ml (5 fl oz/²⁄₃ cup) single (light) cream
625 ml (20 fl oz/2½ cups) cold chicken stock
dash Tabasco sauce
salt and pepper
½ avocado, diced, and snipped fresh chives, to garnish

Halve avocados, discard stones and scoop flesh into a blender or food processor. Add lemon juice, garlic and cream and work to a purée.

Blend in stock and season with Tabasco and salt and pepper.

Turn into a bowl, cover with plastic wrap to prevent discoloration and chill for 1 hour. Serve garnished with diced avocado and snipped chives.

Serves 4-6.

CLEAR BEETROOT SOUP

1 onion, coarsely grated
1 large carrot, coarsely grated
500 g (1 lb) raw beetroot, peeled and coarsely grated
parsley sprig
1 bay leaf
1 litre (1¾ pints/4 cups) chicken stock
1 egg white
juice of ½ lemon
salt and pepper
thin strips lemon peel, to garnish

Put vegetables into a saucepan with herbs and stock. Bring to the boil, then cover and simmer for 30 minutes.

Strain soup and return it to rinsed-out pan. To clear soup, bring to the boil. Whisk egg white, then pour into pan and simmer gently for 15 minutes.

Strain soup through a muslin-lined sieve into a bowl. Add lemon juice, then cool and chill. Season the soup before serving and garnish with thin strips of lemon peel.

Serves 4-6.

VICHYSSOISE

30 g (1 oz/6 teaspoons) butter
3 leeks, trimmed, sliced and washed
1 shallot, finely chopped
250 g (8 oz) potatoes, sliced
785 ml (1 ¼ pints/3 cups) light chicken stock
pinch ground mace or grated nutmeg
salt and pepper
155 ml (5 fl oz/⅔ cup) single (light) cream
snipped fresh chives, to garnish

Melt butter in a large saucepan, add leeks and shallot, then cover and cook gently for 10 minutes without browning. Add potatoes, chicken stock and mace or nutmeg.

Bring to the boil, cover and simmer for 20 minutes. Purée in a blender or food processor, then pass through a sieve. Season with salt and pepper.

Set aside to cool, then stir in two-thirds of the cream. Chill until ready to serve. Ladle into bowls, swirl in remaining cream and garnish with snipped chives.

Serves 6.

— CHILLED SPRING ONION SOUP —

2 bunches spring onions
3 teaspoons olive oil
940 ml (1½ pints/3¾ cups) vegetable stock
salt and pepper
1 hard-boiled egg, shelled, to garnish

Trim green tops from spring onions and set aside. Chop white parts and add to a saucepan with oil, then sauté until soft.

Pour in stock and bring to the boil, then cover and simmer for 15 minutes.

Chop the green parts of onions and add to soup. Cook for just 2 minutes, then set aside to cool. Chill and season with salt and pepper. Chop hard-boiled egg and sprinkle on to the soup to garnish.

Serves 4.

SOUP NORMANDE

30 g (1 oz/6 teaspoons) butter
1 Spanish onion, chopped
1 teaspoon mild curry powder
500 g (1 lb) eating apples
750 ml (24 fl oz/3 cups) chicken stock
2 egg yolks
155 ml (5 fl oz/⅔ cup) double (thick) cream
juice of ½ lemon
salt and pepper
mint leaves, to garnish

Melt butter in a large saucepan, add onion and cook gently until soft. Stir in curry powder.

Reserve 1 apple, then peel, core and chop remainder. Add to pan and cook for 1 minute. Pour in stock and bring to the boil, then cover and simmer for 20 minutes. Purée in a blender or food processor, then return to rinsed-out saucepan.

Beat egg yolks with cream and add to the soup, heating gently until thick. Do not boil. Cool, then chill for at least 2 hours. Peel, core and dice remaining apple and toss in lemon juice. Just before serving, add apple to soup, season and garnish each portion with mint leaves.

Serves 4-6.

COOL CHERRY SOUP

750 g (1½ lb) ripe black or red cherries
155 ml (5 fl oz/⅔ cup) fruity white wine
cinnamon stick
6 teaspoons sugar
grated peel and juice of 1 lemon
315 ml (10 fl oz/1¼ cups) thick sour cream
6 teaspoons brandy (optional)

Stalk and stone the cherries with a stoner, then halve them. Or, halve cherries with a knife and remove stones. Put about half the stones into a strong polythene bag and crush with a mallet.

Put the crushed stones, whole stones and stalks in a saucepan. Add wine, cinnamon stick, sugar, lemon peel and juice and 155 ml (5 fl oz/⅔ cup) water. Bring to the boil, cover and simmer for 10 minutes. Strain and return to the pan with three-quarters of the cherries and simmer for 5 minutes, until softened.

Purée in a blender or food processor. Cool, then whisk in cream, and brandy, if desired, then chill until ready to serve. Serve garnished with the reserved cherries.

Serves 4-6.

WATERCRESS & ALMOND SOUP

2 large bunches watercress
30 g (1 oz/6 teaspoons) butter
1 small onion, finely chopped
500 ml (16 fl oz/2 cups) vegetable stock
60 g (2 oz/⅓ cup) blanched almonds, toasted and
    ground
4 teaspoons cornflour
500 ml (16 fl oz/2 cups) milk
salt and pepper
flaked almonds, lightly toasted, to garnish

Wash watercress and reserve a few sprigs for garnish. Cut away any coarse stalks and chop remainder.

Melt butter in a saucepan, add onion and cook gently until soft. Add watercress and cook for 2 minutes, then stir in stock, cover and simmer for 10 minutes.

Purée in a blender or food processor and return to rinsed out pan with the ground almonds. Blend cornflour with a little of the milk, then add to pan with remaining milk and cook gently over a low heat for 5 minutes, stirring, until smooth. Remove from heat and set aside to cool. Refrigerate for at least 4 hours or overnight. Season, then serve garnished with a few toasted flaked almonds sprinkled on top and the reserved watercress sprigs.

Serves 4.

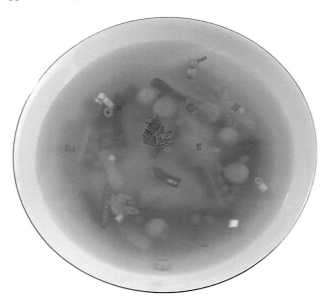

— SUMMER VEGETABLE SOUP —

155 ml (5 fl oz/²⁄₃ cup) tomato juice
625 ml (20 fl oz/2½ cups) clear Vegetable Stock, see
   page 74
grated peel and juice of ½ lemon
2 large carrots
½ red pepper (capsicum), seeded and thinly sliced
½ yellow pepper (capsicum), seeded and thinly sliced
30 g (1 oz) freshly shelled peas
4 spring onions, sliced
chervil leaves, to garnish

Put tomato juice and stock into a large bowl
and whisk in lemon peel and juice. Pour into
a bowl or soup tureen and chill.

Cut out tiny balls from the carrots with a
baller or dice finely. Blanch carrots, peppers
(capsicums) and peas for 2 minutes, then
refresh under cold running water.

Stir vegetables and spring onions into soup.
Chill until ready to serve. Serve garnished
with chervil leaves.

Serves 4.

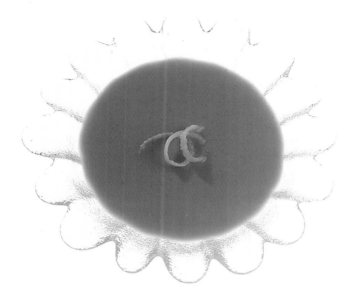

CHILLED PLUM SOUP

500 g (1 lb) red plums
155 ml (5 fl oz/²⁄₃ cup) fruity white wine
60 g (2 oz/¹⁄₃ cup) demerara sugar
3 teaspoons lemon juice
pinch ground cloves
155 ml (5 fl oz/²⁄₃ cup) buttermilk
½ teaspoon grated lemon peel
fine lemon peel twists, to garnish

Combine plums, wine, sugar, lemon juice, ground cloves and 500 ml (16 fl oz/2 cups) water in a saucepan. Bring to the boil, then cover and simmer gently for about 10 minutes, until tender.

Strain through a sieve and discard skin and stones from plums.

Set aside to cool, then stir in buttermilk and lemon peel. Chill the soup in freezer for 1 hour before serving. Serve icy cold, garnished with twists of lemon peel.

Serves 4-6.

PEAR VICHYSSOISE

6 pears
juice of ½ lemon
750 ml (24 fl oz/3 cups) chicken stock
1 leek, white part only, trimmed, chopped and washed
1 potato, chopped
½ teaspoon ground ginger
90 g (3 oz/⅓ cup) low-fat fromage frais
pinch grated nutmeg
salt and pepper
1 pear and watercress sprigs, to garnish

Peel and core the 6 pears, putting fruit into a bowl of water with lemon juice.

Put pear skins and cores into a saucepan with half the stock and simmer for a few minutes to extract all the flavour. Strain into a larger pan. Drain pears, chop coarsely and put into pan with leek, potato, remaining stock and ginger. Bring to the boil, then cover and simmer for 20 minutes, until vegetables are tender.

Purée in a blender or food processor, then pour into a large bowl and set aside to cool, then chill. To serve, whisk fromage frais into the soup, add nutmeg and salt and pepper and garnish with diced or sliced pear and sprigs of watercress.

Serves 4-6.

SENEGALESE SOUP

30 g (1 oz/6 teaspoons) butter
1 small onion, chopped
2 teaspoons mild curry powder
6 teaspoons plain flour
1 litre (1¾ pints/4 cups) chicken stock
juice of ½ lemon
155 ml (5 fl oz/⅔ cup) single (light) cream or natural
   yogurt
125 g (4 oz) cooked skinless chicken breast (fillet), cut
   into thin strips
coriander leaves, to garnish

Melt butter in a saucepan, then add onion and cook gently until soft.

Stir in curry powder and flour and cook for 1 minute. Stir in chicken stock and bring to the boil, then simmer for 4 minutes. Strain soup through a sieve into a bowl. Set aside to cool.

Whisk in lemon juice and cream or yogurt. Stir in chicken and chill for a few hours. Serve well chilled, garnished with coriander leaves.

Serves 4-6.

Variation: Add 125 g (4 oz) peeled cooked prawns, coarsely chopped, instead of the strips of chicken.

— CUCUMBER & YOGURT SOUP —

1 large cucumber
3 teaspoons olive oil
1 small onion, chopped
625 ml (20 fl oz/2½ cups) hot chicken stock
grated peel and juice of ½ lemon
3 teaspoons chopped fresh dill
90 ml (3 fl oz/⅓ cup) strained Greek yogurt
salt and pepper
dill sprigs, to garnish

Cut 5 cm (2 in) piece from cucumber, then chop remainder. Put oil in a pan, add onion and cook gently until soft.

Add chopped cucumber, stock, lemon peel and juice and dill. Bring to the boil, then cover and simmer for 15-20 minutes, until cucumber is tender. Purée in a blender or food processor, then turn into a bowl and cool. Stir in half the yogurt and chill.

Check seasoning, then thinly slice reserved piece of cucumber. Serve the soup garnished with thin slices of cucumber floating on the surface and the remaining yogurt spooned on top with sprigs of dill.

Serves 4-6.

LETTUCE SOUP

2 plain round lettuces
3 teaspoons oil
1 bunch spring onions, about 155 g (5 oz), chopped
1 clove garlic, crushed
500 ml (16 fl oz/2 cups) chicken stock
2 egg yolks
155 ml (5 fl oz/²⁄₃ cup) single (light) cream
salt and pepper

Trim lettuces, discarding any damaged leaves, then separate and wash leaves. Reserve a few for garnish, then shred remaining leaves.

Heat oil in a large saucepan, add spring onions and garlic and cook until tender. Add lettuce, cover and cook until wilted. Pour in stock and bring to the boil. Then re-cover and simmer for 15 minutes. Sieve into a bowl.

Return soup to pan. Beat egg yolks and cream together and stir into soup, then cook over low heat until the soup thickens: do not boil. Cool soup, then chill. To serve, season, then roll up reserved lettuce leaves and slice finely to make a chiffonade. Stir into the soup as a garnish, then serve at once.

Serves 4.

FINNISH BERRY SOUP

750 g (1 ½ lb) fresh or frozen mixed berries, such as
  raspberries, redcurrants, blackcurrants
250 ml (8 fl oz/1 cup) sweet white wine
cinnamon stick
60 g (2 oz/¼ cup) sugar
125 ml (4 fl oz/½ cup) whipping cream, to garnish

Select a few of the best raspberries for
garnishing and reserve. Put remaining fruit in
a pan with the wine, cinnamon stick, sugar
and 500 ml (16 fl oz/2 cups) water. Simmer for
5-10 minutes, stirring occasionally, until fruit
is soft.

Discard cinnamon stick and strain the soup
through a fine sieve.

Cool, then chill for at least 1 hour before
serving. To serve, lightly whip the cream and
swirl on to the soup, then top with the
reserved raspberries.

Serves 6.

ICED FENNEL SOUP

2 fennel bulbs, about 500 g (1 lb)
3 teaspoons sunflower oil
1 small onion, chopped
785 ml (1 ¼ pints/3 cups) chicken or vegetable stock
155 ml (5 fl oz/²⁄₃ cup) thick sour cream
salt and pepper

Remove the green feathery fronds from fennel and reserve. Roughly chop bulbs. Put oil into a saucepan over a medium heat, add fennel and onion, then cover and cook gently for 10 minutes.

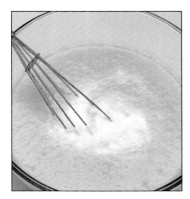

Add stock and bring to the boil, then reduce heat and simmer for about 20 minutes or until the fennel is tender.

Purée the soup in a blender or food processor. Cool, then whisk in sour cream and season with salt and pepper. Chill and check seasoning again before serving, garnished with reserved fennel fronds.

Serves 6.

— PROVENÇAL FISH CHOWDER —

60 ml (2 fl oz/¼ cup) virgin olive oil
1 small onion, finely chopped
1 leek, trimmed and finely sliced
2 cloves garlic, crushed
375 g (12 oz) ripe tomatoes, skinned and diced
bouquet garni
1 bay leaf
250 g (8 oz) potatoes, diced
1.5 litres (2½ pints/6 cups) fish stock
3 teaspoons tomato purée (paste)
750 g (1½ lb) white fish, such as cod, skinned and
    boned
½ teaspoon dried basil
60 g (2 oz) small black olives, stoned and halved
salt and pepper

Heat oil in a large saucepan, add onion, leek
and garlic and cook gently for 5 minutes,
until softened. Add tomatoes and cook for
about 10 minutes, until soft. Add bouquet
garni, bay leaf, potatoes, stock and tomato
purée (paste), cover and simmer for 15
minutes, until potatoes are just tender.

Cut fish into 4 cm (1½ in) pieces and add to
soup with basil and olives. Season, then
remove bouquet garni and bay leaf before
serving.

Serves 4-6.

CREAMY FISH SOUP

375 g (12 oz) white fish fillets, skinned
45 g (1½ oz/9 teaspoons) butter
45 g (1½ oz/⅓ cup) plain flour
155 ml (5 fl oz/⅔ cup) single (light) cream
salt
chopped fresh parsley and paprika, to garnish

FISH STOCK: 500 g (1lb) fish heads, bones and
    trimmings
1 small onion, quartered
1 carrot, sliced
1 stick celery, chopped
bouquet garni
salt and 6 black peppercorns
1 bay leaf
1 lemon slice

To make stock, place fish bits, vegetables and
bouquet garni in a large saucepan. Pour in 1.2
litres (2 pints/5 cups) water and add salt,
peppercorns, bay leaf and lemon slice. Bring
to the boil over a low heat, skim off any scum
that rises to surface, then simmer for 20
minutes. Strain the stock, without pressing,
through a muslin-lined colander into a bowl.
Measure 940 ml (1½ pints/3¾ cups) of the
stock into a pan (freeze remainder). Add fish
fillets and poach until flaking.

Transfer fish to a blender or food processor
with a little cooking liquid and purée. Melt
butter in a pan, stir in flour and cook for 1
minute without browning. Gradually add
remaining cooking liquid, then return to heat
and stir until boiling. Simmer for 10 minutes.
Then whisk in puréed fish, and cream; season
if necessary. Serve garnished with chopped
parsley and paprika.

Serves 4-6.

— SMOKED HADDOCK CHOWDER —

500 g (1 lb) smoked haddock fillets, skinned
30 g (1 oz/6 teaspoons) butter
1 onion, chopped
500 ml (16 fl oz/2 cups) fish stock
250 g (8 oz) potato, diced
1 carrot, diced
1 bay leaf
4 teaspoons cornflour
625 ml (20 fl oz/2 ½ cups) milk
60 g (2 oz/1 cup) fresh white breadcrumbs
squeeze lemon juice
pepper
chopped fresh parsley, to garnish

Cut fish into 2.5 cm (1 in) pieces.

Melt butter in a saucepan, add onion and cook over a gentle heat until soft. Add stock, potato, carrot and bay leaf, then cover and simmer for 15 minutes, until potatoes are just tender.

Blend cornflour with a little of the milk, then add to soup with remaining milk and fish. Simmer gently for 8-10 minutes, until the fish is cooked: do not boil or fish will disintegrate. Remove bay leaf, stir in breadcrumbs and season with lemon juice and pepper. Serve garnished with chopped parsley.

Serves 6.

MUSSEL CHOWDER

1 kg (2 lb) fresh mussels, well scrubbed with beards
   removed
3 teaspoons olive oil
1 small onion, finely chopped
1 small green pepper (capsicum), seeded and chopped
1 clove garlic, crushed
375 g (12 oz) ripe tomatoes, skinned and chopped
1 bay leaf
1 teaspoon dried thyme
salt and pepper
chopped fresh parsley, to garnish, if desired

Discard any mussels that are open. Put
remainder in a large pan with 315 ml (10 fl
oz/1¼ cups) water.

Cover and bring to boil. Cook gently, shaking
pan once during cooking, until mussel shells
have opened. Drain mussels, reserving
liquid, and discard any that are unopened.
Shell remainder, reserving 8 small mussels in
shells for garnish. Heat oil in a pan, add
onion, pepper (capsicum) and garlic and
cook gently for 5 minutes, until softened.
Add tomatoes, bay leaf and thyme; season
then cook for 3 minutes.

Make reserved cooking liquid up to 625 ml
(20 fl oz/2½ cups) with water if necessary and
pour into pan. Simmer, covered, for 15
minutes. Add shelled mussels, cook for 5
minutes, then remove bay leaf and check
seasoning. Ladle into serving bowls, sprinkle
over parsley, if desired, and garnish with
reserved mussels in their shells.

Serves 4.

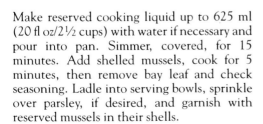

CREAM OF PRAWN SOUP

500 g (1 lb) raw prawns
60 g (2 oz/¼ cup) butter
1 small onion, chopped
45 g (1 ½ oz/⅓ cup) plain flour
9 teaspoons white wine
155 ml (5 fl oz/⅔ cup) single (light) cream

SHELLFISH STOCK: 250 g (8 oz) fish scraps and bones
1 strip lemon peel
1 stick celery, chopped
1 small onion, quartered
5 fennel seeds
salt and pepper

Peel prawns and set aside. To make stock, put prawn shells into a large saucepan with 1.2 litres (2 pints/5 cups) water and remaining stock ingredients and slowly bring to the boil, removing any scum which rises to surface. Lower heat and simmer for 25 minutes, then strain through a muslin-lined sieve. Return to rinsed-out pan and simmer to reduce to 750 ml (24 fl oz/3 cups).

Melt butter in a saucepan, add onion and cook until soft. Stir in flour, cook for 1 minute, then gradually blend in stock. Add wine and three-quarters of the prawns, bring to the boil, then simmer for 10 minutes. Cool soup slightly, then purée in a blender or food processor. Return to pan and add cream and salt and pepper if necessary. Reheat gently for 3-4 minutes, then serve, garnished with reserved prawns.

Serves 4.

CARIBBEAN FISH SOUP

375 g (12 oz) fresh tuna or swordfish steaks
juice of 1 lime
1 green chilli, seeded and finely chopped
2 cloves garlic, crushed
6 teaspoons sunflower oil
1 small onion, finely chopped
1 green pepper (capsicum), seeded and diced
1 red pepper (capsicum), seeded and diced
155 ml (5 fl oz/^{2}/$_3$ cup) dry white wine
750 ml (24 fl oz/3 cups) fish stock
1 teaspoon demerara sugar
2 tomatoes, skinned and diced
1 small ripe mango, peeled and diced
salt and pepper

Cut the fish into 2.5 cm (1 in) pieces and put into a glass dish. Pour over lime juice and stir in chilli and garlic, then cover and leave to marinate for 1 hour. Heat oil in a saucepan, add onion and peppers (capsicums) and cook for 5 minutes over medium heat, until softened. Add wine, stock and sugar, cover and simmer for 15 minutes.

Stir in tomatoes, mango and fish with marinade and simmer gently for a further 10 minutes, until fish is cooked through. Season to taste and serve hot.

Serves 4-6.

SOUPE DE POISSONS

75 ml (2½ fl oz/⅓ cup) olive oil
2 leeks, white part only, trimmed and sliced
1.25 kg (2½ lb) mixture of fish
250 g (8 oz) small unpeeled shrimps
2 cloves garlic, chopped
500 g (1 lb) ripe tomatoes, chopped
bouquet garni and salt and pepper
1.5 litres (2½ pints/6 cups) fish stock or water
slices of oven-dried French stick and Gruyère cheese,
    grated, to garnish

ROUILLE: 2 slices bread, soaked in milk
3 cloves garlic
1 teaspoon paprika and ¼ teaspoon cayenne
75 ml (2½ fl oz/⅓ cup) olive oil
4 teaspoons tomato purée (paste)

To make rouille, squeeze milk from bread, put
into a mortar with garlic and pound to a
paste. Add paprika and cayenne, then add oil
drop by drop until blended. Beat in tomato
purée (paste). To make soup, heat oil in a
very large saucepan, add leeks and cook until
soft. Stir in fish and shrimps and turn in oil
over a high heat until it starts to colour. Add
garlic and tomatoes, cover and cook gently
10 minutes. Add bouquet garni and stock or
water. Bring to the boil, then cover and
simmer 30 minutes.

Discard bouquet garni and strain the soup
into a bowl. Put solids in a blender with a
little of the fish stock and purée. Press the
mixture through a sieve into the bowl. Add 4
or 5 tablespoons fish soup to rouille and mix
until smooth. Return soup to pan and reheat.
Add salt and pepper if necessary. Serve hot
with rouille spread on the slices of toast,
topped with grated Gruyère cheese.

Serves 6-8.

NEW ENGLAND CLAM CHOWDER

two 315 g (10 oz) cans clams
90 g (3 oz) back bacon, rinded and diced
1 onion, finely chopped
500 g (1 lb) potatoes, diced
315 ml (10 fl oz/1¼ cups) fish stock
315 ml (10 fl oz/1¼ cups) milk
155 ml (5 fl oz/⅔ cup) single (light) cream
pinch dried thyme
salt and pepper
fresh thyme leaves or paprika to garnish

Drain clams, reserving liquid, then chop and set aside.

Put bacon into a saucepan and fry over high heat until fat runs and bacon is lightly browned. Add onion and cook until soft, then add potatoes, liquid from clams, fish stock and milk. Bring to the boil, then cover and simmer for about 20 minutes, or until potatoes are tender.

Stir in cream, clams, thyme and salt and pepper, then reheat for a few minutes: do not boil. Serve garnished with thyme or paprika.

Serves 6.

SHRIMP BISQUE

250 g (8 oz) unpeeled shrimps
60 g (2 oz/¼ cup) butter
1 small onion, finely chopped
155 ml (5 fl oz/⅔ cup) dry white wine
1 fish stock cube
1 bay leaf
few parsley stalks
3 strips lemon peel
3 teaspoons tomato purée (paste)
salt and pepper
30 g (1 oz/¼ cup) plain flour
grated nutmeg
155 ml (5 fl oz/⅔ cup) single (light) cream

Peel a few shrimps and reserve for garnish.

Process remainder in a blender or food processor until finely chopped. Melt half the butter in a saucepan, add onion and cook gently until soft. Stir in shrimps, cook for 4-5 minutes, then add wine and boil 2 minutes. Add 940 ml (1½ pints/3¾ cups) water, stock cube, bay leaf, parsley stalks, lemon peel, tomato purée (paste) and salt and pepper and bring to the boil. Simmer, uncovered, for 30 minutes, skimming surface. Strain through a nylon sieve. Discard bay leaf and parsley stalks, then put remaining solids in a blender or food processor with a little cooking liquid.

Work to make a purée. Press purée through a sieve into the cooking stock. Melt remaining butter in a clean pan, add flour and cook for 1 minute. Gradually stir in fish soup and season with nutmeg and salt and pepper. Bring to the boil, stirring constantly and simmer for 3 minutes, then stir in half the cream. Serve with remaining cream swirled on top and garnished with reserved shrimps scattered over.

Serves 4.

BOURRIDE

1 kg (2 lb) firm white fish
2 leeks, trimmed and sliced
2 cloves garlic
2 tomatoes, chopped
1 orange peel strip
bouquet garni
155 ml (5 fl oz/²⁄₃ cup) dry white wine
940 ml (1½ pints/3¾ cups) fish stock
4 egg yolks
½ French stick, sliced, to garnish

AÏOLI: 4 cloves garlic
2 egg yolks
salt
315 ml (10 fl oz/1¼ cups) olive oil

To make aïoli, put garlic into a mortar and pound to a pulp. Beat in egg yolks with a pinch of salt and start adding oil drop by drop. When one-third has been used, add remainder more quickly, until thick. To make soup, clean fish and cut into good size pieces. Put leeks, garlic, tomatoes, peel and bouquet garni into a large pan. Add fish, then pour over wine and stock and season with salt. Bring to the boil, then cook gently for 10-15 minutes, until fish is cooked through. Remove fish and keep warm.

Strain stock into a jug. Put half of the aïoli in a bowl and beat in the 4 egg yolks, then pour in hot stock, whisking constantly. Return to rinsed-out pan and stir over low heat until slightly thick: do not boil. To serve, toast bread slices and arrange in each soup bowl with pieces of fish, then pour over soup. Extra slices of bread spread with the remaining aïoli can be served separately.

Serves 6.

TUNA & CORN BISQUE

30 g (1 oz/6 teaspoons) butter
1 small onion, finely chopped
1 teaspoon mild curry powder
1 teaspoon paprika
30 g (1 oz/¼ cup) plain flour
500 ml (16 fl oz/2 cups) chicken stock
500 ml (16 fl oz/2 cups) milk
grated peel of ½ lemon
375 g (12 oz) can sweetcorn, drained
220 g (7 oz) can tuna, drained
3 teaspoons chopped fresh parsley
60 g (2 oz/½ cup) Cheddar cheese, grated, to garnish

Melt butter in a saucepan and add onion.

Cook onion gently until soft. Stir in curry powder, paprika and flour and cook for 1 minute, stirring. Gradually stir in stock and bring to the boil, stirring constantly. Add milk, lemon peel and sweetcorn and simmer for 5 minutes.

Stir in tuna, breaking it up into flakes and simmer for a further 5 minutes. Sprinkle in parsley and garnish with a little pile of grated cheese in the middle of each serving.

Serves 4.

— ARTICHOKE & SCALLOP SOUP —

625 g (1¼ lb) Jerusalem artichokes
3 teaspoons lemon juice
60 g (2 oz/¼ cup) butter
1 small onion, chopped
625 ml (20 fl oz/2½ cups) chicken stock
315 ml (10 fl oz/1¼ cups) milk
1 potato, diced
6 scallops
salt and pepper
60 ml (2 fl oz/¼ cup) double (thick) cream
fresh chervil leaves, to garnish

Peel and slice artichokes, then put in a bowl of water with lemon juice.

Melt three-quarters of the butter in a saucepan. Drain artichokes and add to pan with onion, then cover and cook gently for 10 minutes. Add stock, milk and potato and bring to the boil, then cover and simmer for 15-20 minutes, until artichokes are soft. Purée in a blender or food processor and return to pan.

Cut white parts of scallops into small pieces and add to soup with milk. Simmer for a few minutes, then season. Melt remaining butter in a small frying pan and gently sauté scallop corals until firm. Slice each in half. Just before serving soup, add cream and gently heat through. Serve garnished with corals and chervil leaves.

Serves 4.

— VIETNAMESE PRAWN SOUP —

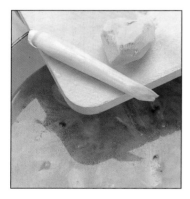

250 g (8 oz) unpeeled cooked prawns
1 bulb lemon grass, split in half lengthwise
5 cm (2 in) piece fresh root ginger, peeled
940 ml (1½ pints/3¾ cups) light chicken stock
3 teaspoons lime juice
½ teaspoon crushed dried chillies or ¼ teaspoon
    minced red chilli relish
3 teaspoons nam pla (fish sauce) or 3 teaspoons soy
    sauce
125 g (4 oz) bok choi leaves, finely shredded

Peel prawns and set aside. Put shells in a saucepan with lemon grass, ginger and stock. Bring to boil, then simmer for 5 minutes. Set aside for 15 minutes, covered.

Strain stock into a bowl, then return to pan. Add lime juice, chillies or relish, nam pla or soy sauce and bok choi. Simmer for 2 minutes.

Add prawns and simmer gently for 1 minute. Serve at once.

Serves 4.

CRAB & SWEETCORN SOUP

940 ml (1½ pints/3¾ cups) chicken stock
1 small knob fresh root ginger, peeled
2 teaspoons light soy sauce
3 teaspoons dry sherry
470 g (15 oz) can creamed sweetcorn
salt and pepper
2 teaspoons cornflour
125 g (4 oz) crabmeat, well drained if canned
2 eggs, beaten
2 spring onions, finely chopped, to garnish

Put stock into a saucepan with ginger, cover and simmer for 15 minutes. Remove ginger, then stir in soy sauce, sherry, sweetcorn and salt and pepper and simmer for 5 minutes.

Blend cornflour with 6 teaspoons water and stir into soup with crabmeat, stirring over medium heat until thickened.

With soup at a gentle simmer, slowly pour in beaten eggs in a thin stream, stirring constantly: do not boil. Serve garnished with chopped spring onions.

Serves 4-6.

STRACCIATELLA

1.2 litres (2 pints/5 cups) well-flavoured chicken stock
2 eggs
22 g (¾ oz/9 teaspoons) freshly grated Parmesan
   cheese
3 teaspoons semolina
2 teaspoons chopped fresh parsley
pinch grated nutmeg
salt

Put stock in a pan and begin to bring to the boil. Meanwhile, beat eggs and add cheese, semolina, parsley, nutmeg and salt together in a bowl.

When the chicken stock comes to a bubbling boil, carefully pour in egg mixture, stirring constantly.

Lower heat and simmer for 2-3 minutes. The egg will form long threads but may look like small flakes in the stock. Serve at once.

Serves 4.

CELERY & STILTON SOUP

1 head celery
45 g (1½ oz/9 teaspoons) butter
1 onion, chopped
940 ml (1½ pints/3¾ cups) light vegetable or chicken
    stock
2 egg yolks
155 ml (5 fl oz/⅔ cup) single (light) cream
125 g (4 oz) blue Stilton, rinded and crumbled
salt and pepper

BLUE CHEESE CROÛTONS: 30 g (1 oz/6 teaspoons) butter,
    softened
30 g (1 oz) blue cheese, grated
1 thick slice bread

Reserve inner leaves from celery and chop remainder. Melt butter in a large saucepan, add celery and onion, then cover and cook gently, until soft. Add stock, bring to the boil, re-cover and simmer 20 minutes or until vegetables are tender. Cool slightly, then purée in a blender or food processor. Return soup to rinsed-out pan and reheat gently: do not boil.

Meanwhile, make croûtons. Beat butter and cheese together. Toast bread and spread cheese butter on 1 side, then grill until melted. Cut into squares. To finish soup, beat egg yolks and cream together. Stir a small ladleful of soup into egg mixture and pour back into pan. Stir in cheese, stirring until thick. Season if needed. Serve hot with croûtons and garnished with reserved celery leaves.

Serves 4-6.

— POTAGE CRÈME DE FROMAGE —

30 g (1 oz/6 teaspoons) butter
1 onion, finely chopped
1 stick celery, finely chopped
30 g (1 oz/¼ cup) plain flour
500 ml (16 fl oz/2 cups) hot chicken stock
155 ml (5 fl oz/⅔ cup) milk
125 g (4 oz) camembert, rind removed
125 g (4 oz/½ cup) fromage frais
salt and pepper

PARSLEY CROÙTONS: 1 thick slice white bread, crusts
    removed
butter
2 tablespoons finely chopped fresh parsley

Melt butter in a saucepan, add onion and celery and cook gently for 5 minutes, until soft. Stir in flour and cook for 1 minute. Gradually stir in stock and milk, then return to a low heat and simmer for 15 minutes. Meanwhile, make croûtons. Toast bread on both sides until golden. Set aside to cool, then butter. Cut into small squares and then toss in parsley.

Cut the camembert into small pieces and add to soup with fromage frais. Stir for 2-3 minutes, until camembert melts. Add salt and pepper. Serve garnished with parsley croûtons.

Serves 4.

PAVIA SOUP

1.2 litres (2 pints/5 cups) Chicken Consommé, see
   page 96
60-90 g (2-3 oz/¼-⅓ cup) butter
2 slices firm bread
60 g (2 oz/½ cup) freshly grated Parmesan cheese
12 quail eggs
flat-leaf parsley, to garnish

Put consommé into a saucepan and bring to
simmering point. Melt butter in a frying pan.
Fry the bread on both sides until golden, then
cut into 12 pieces. Sprinkle with grated
cheese and set aside.

Carefully break quail eggs into consommé,
cooking 3 or 4 at a time. As soon as they are
set, lift out with a slotted spoon and put on
pieces of fried bread. Repeat until all the eggs
are cooked.

To serve, place 3 pieces of bread in each soup
plate and strain hot consommé over. Garnish
with flat-leaf parsley and serve extra grated
Parmesan cheese, if desired.

Serves 4.

OMELETTE SOUP

1.2 litres (2 pints/5 cups) chicken stock
3 eggs
3 teaspoons plain flour
90 ml (3 fl oz/⅓ cup) milk
salt
vegetable oil or butter for frying
15 g (½ oz/6 teaspoons) freshly grated Parmesan
   cheese

Put stock into a saucepan and begin to bring
to the boil. Beat eggs, flour, milk and salt
together.

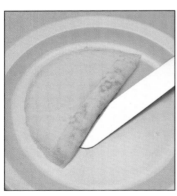

Lightly grease bottom of an 18 cm (7 in)
frying pan and pour in one third of egg
mixture and make an omelette, cooking until
set and golden. Turn out on to a plate and roll
up like a Swiss roll. Repeat the process with
remaining egg mixture to make a total of 3
omelettes.

Cut omelettes across into thin strips. Add to
the soup, reheat gently and serve sprinkled
with grated Parmesan cheese.

Serves 4.

AVGOLEMONO

1.2 litres (2 pints/5 cups) chicken stock
salt and pepper
60 g (2 oz/⅓ cup) long-grain rice
2 eggs
finely grated peel of ½ lemon
juice of 1 lemon
3 tablespoons chopped fresh parsley
parsley sprigs and thin lemon slices, to garnish

Put stock into a saucepan and bring to the boil. Add salt and pepper and rice and simmer for 15 minutes or until rice is tender.

Break the eggs into a bowl, add lemon peel and juice and beat together. Whisk in a ladleful of hot stock, then pour mixture back into pan, stirring constantly.

Reheat over a low heat until the soup thickens and looks creamy: do not boil. Stir in chopped parsley and serve at once, garnished with a parsley sprig and a lemon slice on each portion.

Serves 4-6.

Note: This soup can also be served cold.

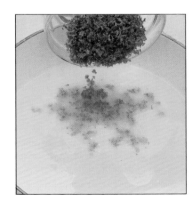

PLOUGHMAN'S SOUP

45 g (1½ oz/9 teaspoons) butter
2 onions, chopped
30 g (1 oz/¼ cup) plain wholemeal flour
500 ml (16 fl oz/2 cups) chicken stock
250 ml (8 fl oz/1 cup) light ale
dash Worcestershire sauce
185 g (6 oz) Cheshire cheese, crumbled
salt and pepper
mild raw onion rings, to garnish

Melt butter in a saucepan, add onions and cook gently until soft. Stir in flour and cook for 1 minute. Remove from heat.

Gradually stir in stock and ale, then return to heat. Bring to the boil and simmer 5 minutes, until thickened. Flavour with Worcestershire sauce.

Stir in cheese a little at a time over a low heat, until melted, then add salt and pepper. Serve garnished with onion rings.

Serves 4.

PASSATELLI

940 ml (30 fl oz/3¾ cups) well-flavoured chicken
    stock
4 eggs
125 g (4 oz/1 cup) freshly grated Parmesan cheese
125 g (4 oz/1 cup) fine dry white breadcrumbs
¼ teaspoon grated nutmeg
30 g (1 oz/6 teaspoons) butter, softened
salt and pepper

Bring stock to the boil in a large saucepan.

Break the eggs into a bowl and beat together,
then add cheese, breadcrumbs, nutmeg and
butter. Season with salt and pepper. Mix to
make a stiff paste.

Put paste into a colander and press through
into boiling stock. Simmer for 1-2 minutes,
until the threads of noodles rise to the
surface, then remove from the heat and leave
to stand for 5 minutes before serving.

Serves 4.

FENNEL & WALNUT SOUP

3 teaspoons vegetable oil
1 onion, chopped
1 large bulb fennel, trimmed and chopped
940 ml (1½ pints/3¾ cups) vegetable stock
60 g (2 oz/½ cup) chopped walnuts

SAGE DERBY PUFFS: 30 g (1 oz/6 teaspoons) butter
30 g (1 oz/¼ cup) plain flour
½ egg, beaten
90 g (3 oz) Sage Derby cheese grated
salt and pepper
60 g (2 oz/¼ cup) cream cheese
6 teaspoons single (light) cream

To make puffs, preheat oven to 200C (400F/ Gas 6). Put butter and 45 ml (1½ fl oz/9 teaspoons) water into a saucepan and bring to the boil. Add flour off heat and beat until smooth. Cool slightly, then beat in egg and add half Sage Derby and salt and pepper. Put into a piping bag fitted with small plain nozzle and pipe blobs the size of peas on to a greased baking tray. Bake 7-10 minutes, until crisp. Cool slightly, then slit each. To make soup, heat oil in a pan, add onion and fennel and cook until soft. Add stock, bring to boil, then simmer, covered, for 20 minutes.

Meanwhile, beat remaining cheese with cream cheese and cream. Fill pastry puffs. Grind three-quarters of the walnuts in a blender or food processor; chop the rest and reserve for garnish. Purée soup until smooth, then return to pan and stir in ground nuts and add salt and pepper. Reheat gently. Serve garnished with Sage Derby puffs and sprinkled with reserved walnuts.

Serves 4-6.

CHICKEN EGG DROP SOUP

5 teaspoons cornflour
9 teaspoons rice wine
3 teaspoons soy sauce
1.2 litres (2 pints/5 cups) chicken stock
½ teaspoon sugar
250 g (8 oz) cooked and skinned chicken breast (fillet),
    diced
6 spring onions, shredded
2 eggs
4 teaspoons plain flour
spring onion curls, to garnish

Put cornflour in a saucepan; blend in rice wine and soy sauce. Add stock and sugar and bring to the boil, then simmer 2 minutes.

Add chicken and shredded spring onions and continue simmering for 2-3 minutes.

Beat eggs together with flour. While soup is simmering, pour egg mixture through a sieve into the pan and continue simmering for 1 minute, stirring as egg drops into the pan. Serve garnished with spring onion curls.

Serves 4-6.

TOMATO & RICE SOUP

1 small onion, chopped
2 cloves garlic, crushed
794 g (1 lb 12 oz) can tomatoes
6 teaspoons tomato purée (paste)
3 teaspoons chopped fresh basil or ½ teaspoon dried
1 teaspoon sugar
60 g (2 oz/⅓ cup) long-grain rice
9 teaspoons dry sherry
salt and pepper
9 teaspoons single (light) cream and basil leaves, to
   garnish, if desired

Put onion, garlic, tomatoes with their juice, tomato purée (paste), basil, sugar and 625 ml (20 fl oz/2½ cups) water into a saucepan. Bring to the boil, cover and simmer for 30 minutes. Pour into a blender or food processor and purée. Sieve purée back into pan.

Bring back to the boil, then add rice, lower heat and simmer for 15 minutes, until rice is tender. Stir in sherry and salt and pepper. Serve in individual bowls, garnished with a swirl of cream and basil leaves, if desired.

Serves 4-6.

– COUNTRY MUSHROOM SOUP –

1 onion, thinly sliced
60 g (2 oz/⅓ cup) brown rice
1.5 litres (2½ pints/6 cups) chicken stock
45 g (1½ oz/9 teaspoons) butter
500 g (1 lb) mushrooms, wiped, trimmed and sliced
75 ml (2½ fl oz/⅓ cup) dry sherry
salt and pepper
parsley sprigs, to garnish

Put onion, rice and stock in a large saucepan and bring to the boil, then simmer for 25 minutes, until rice is tender.

Meanwhile, melt butter in another pan, add mushrooms and cook gently for about 10 minutes, until golden brown and most of the moisture has evaporated.

Transfer the mushrooms to stock, stir in sherry and season with salt and pepper. Simmer for 10 minutes, then serve garnished with sprigs of parsley.

Serves 6.

Variation: Use 2 varieties of mushrooms if available, such as button and open or chestnut mushrooms which have very good flavours. If wild mushrooms are available they can also be used.

— ROSEMARY & LENTIL SOUP —

185 g (6 oz) green lentils, soaked overnight
1.9 litres (3 pints/7 ½ cups) vegetable stock
1 potato, diced
2 sticks celery, diced
1 clove garlic, crushed
large sprig fresh rosemary
salt and pepper
fresh rosemary sprigs, to garnish

SAUSAGE DUMPLINGS: 90 g (3 oz) pork sausagemeat
30 g (1 oz/¼ cup) plain flour
½ teaspoon mixed dried herbs
½ small egg, beaten

Drain lentils and put into a large saucepan with stock. Slowly bring to the boil, skim off any scum which rises to the surface and simmer for 15 minutes. Add potato, celery, garlic and rosemary. Season with salt and pepper, then cover and simmer for 30 minutes. Remove rosemary, then purée the soup in a blender or food processor.

Return soup to pan and reheat slowly while making dumplings. Put all dumpling ingredients into a bowl and mix together with a palette knife. Divide mixture into small heaps. When soup is simmering, drop dumplings into the pan, keeping them apart. Cover and continue cooking for 15 minutes. Serve the soup garnished with rosemary.

Serves 6.

— ITALIAN BEAN & PASTA SOUP —

6 teaspoons olive oil
1 onion, finely chopped
1 clove garlic, crushed
2 sticks celery, finely sliced
1 carrot, finely diced
3 teaspoons tomato purée (paste)
1.2 litres (2 pints/5 cups) beef stock
470 g (15 oz) can borlotti beans, drained and rinsed
90 g (3 oz) small pasta shapes
125 g (4 oz) shelled peas
salt and pepper

Heat oil in a large saucepan, add onion, garlic, celery and carrot.

Cook gently 5 minutes, until soft. Add tomato purée (paste), stock and beans and bring to the boil, then simmer 10 minutes.

Add pasta and peas and cook a further 7 minutes, until the pasta is just cooked. Add salt and pepper and serve hot.

Serves 4-6.

SPICY LENTIL SOUP

6 teaspoons olive oil
½ teaspoon cumin seeds
1 onion, chopped
1 clove garlic, crushed
2 carrots, chopped
2 sticks celery, chopped
½ teaspoon chilli powder
½ teaspoon turmeric
1 teaspoon ground coriander
185 g (6 oz) red lentils, washed and picked over
1.2 litres (2 pints/5 cups) vegetable stock
1 bay leaf
salt and pepper
fried onion rings and coriander leaves, to garnish

Heat oil in a saucepan over a medium heat; add cumin seeds. As soon as seeds begin to pop, add onion and cook until golden, stirring. Add garlic, carrots and celery and cook gently for 10 minutes, until soft. Stir in all the spices and cook for a further 1 minute before adding lentils.

Pour in stock and bay leaf and bring to the boil, then simmer for 1 hour, skimming surface if necessary. Remove bay leaf and purée soup in a blender or food processor. Return to pan, season with salt and pepper and reheat. Serve garnished with fried onion rings and coriander leaves.

Serves 6.

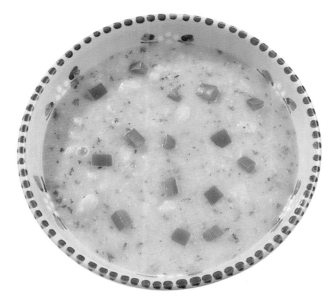

WHITE BEAN SOUP

250 g (8 oz) haricot or cannellini beans, soaked
  overnight
940 ml (1 ½ pints/3 ¾ cups) chicken stock
salt and pepper
6 teaspoons olive oil
1 clove garlic, crushed
2 tablespoons chopped fresh parsley

TO GARNISH: 1 tablespoon diced red pepper (capsicum)
1 tablespoon diced green pepper (capsicum)
extra olive oil, if desired

Drain the beans and put into a large pan with
stock and 940 ml (1½ pints/3¾ cups) water.

Bring to the boil, then half cover and simmer
for 2-2½ hours, until beans are tender,
skimming surface if necessary. Press half of
the beans through a sieve or purée in a
blender or food processor. Stir purée back
into soup and add salt and pepper.

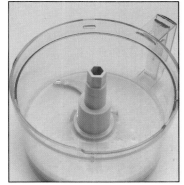

Heat oil in a small pan, add garlic and cook
gently until soft: do not brown. Stir into soup
with parsley. Reheat gently. Meanwhile,
bring a small pan of water to the boil, then
add peppers (capsicums) and blanch for 2
minutes. Drain. Serve soup garnished with
peppers (capsicums). A little extra olive oil
can be poured over the surface, if desired.

Serves 4-6.

BLACK BEAN SOUP

250 g (8 oz) dried black beans
6 teaspoons vegetable oil
1 onion, finely chopped
1 bay leaf
1.2 litres (2 pints/5 cups) vegetable or chicken stock
1 green or yellow pepper (capsicum), seeded and diced
2 cloves garlic, crushed
60 g (2 oz/¹⁄₃ cup) brown rice
125 g (4 oz) diced cooked ham
salt and pepper

Wash and pick over the beans, then put into a saucepan with enough water to cover.

Bring to the boil and boil for 2 minutes, then cover and set aside to stand for 2 hours. Drain well. Heat oil in a pan, add onion and cook until browned. Add bay leaf, beans and 1.2 litres (2 pints/5 cups) water and bring to the boil, then cover and simmer for 1½ hours.

Drain beans and onion, then put into a pan with stock, pepper, (capsicum), garlic and rice. Add salt and pepper and simmer for 1 hour, or until the beans are tender. Add ham and season if necessary before serving.

Serves 4-6.

DUTCH PEA SOUP

250 g (8 oz) yellow split peas, soaked overnight
bouquet garni
1 bay leaf
250 g (8 oz) back bacon, diced
1 onion, chopped
2 leeks, trimmed and chopped
1 large carrot, chopped
2 sticks celery, chopped
salt and pepper
125 g (4 oz) pieces spicy or garlic sausage, diced
2 tablespoons chopped fresh parsley

Drain peas and put into a large pan with
bouquet garni, bay leaf and 1.5 litres (2½
pints/6 cups) water.

Bring to the boil, then cover and simmer for 2
hours, skimming surface if necessary. Add
bacon and vegetables, then simmer for a
further 1 hour.

Remove bouquet garni and bay leaf and purée
the soup in a blender or food processor.
Return to pan and add salt and pepper and
sausage. Reheat, then stir in parsley and
serve.

Serves 6.

MEXICAN BEAN SOUP

6 teaspoons olive oil
1 onion, chopped
1 clove garlic, crushed
1 green pepper (capsicum), seeded and diced
375 g (12 oz) tomatoes, skinned and chopped
½ teaspoon chilli powder
940 ml (1½ pints/3¾ cups) vegetable stock
6 teaspoons tomato purée (paste)
470 g (15 oz) can red kidney beans, drained
salt and pepper
125 g (4 oz) canned sweetcorn
1 avocado
few drops Tabasco sauce
1 tablespoon chopped fresh coriander
coriander leaves, to garnish

Heat oil in a large saucepan and cook onion until soft. Add garlic, green pepper (capsicum), tomatoes and chilli powder and cook for 3-4 minutes. Pour in stock with tomato purée (paste) and three-quarters of the beans. Re-cover and simmer for 30 minutes, then cool slightly and purée in a blender or food processor.

Return to pan and add salt and pepper, remaining beans and sweetcorn. Peel and dice avocado and add with the Tabasco sauce. Reheat gently, stir in coriander and serve garnished with coriander leaves.

Serves 4-5.

—— HARVEST BARLEY SOUP ——

60 g (2 oz/⅓ cup) pearl barley
1.2 litres (2 pints/5 cups) vegetable stock
1 large carrot, diced
1 small turnip, diced
1 stick celery, chopped
1 small onion, finely chopped
2 young leeks, trimmed and sliced
½ teaspoon mixed dried herbs and 1 bay leaf
5 teaspoons tomato purée (paste)
salt and pepper
230 g (7½ oz) can butter beans, drained and rinsed

CHEESY CROÛTONS: 1 thick slice bread
60 g (2 oz/½ cup) Cheddar cheese, grated

Put barley into a saucepan with stock and bring to the boil, then cover and simmer for 45 minutes, until barley is tender. Add vegetables, herbs, tomato purée (paste) and salt and pepper and simmer, covered, for 20 minutes. Meanwhile, make croûtons. Toast bread on both sides, remove crusts and scatter cheese over the bread. Grill until melted and golden. Cut into squares.

Remove bay leaf from soup, stir in beans and cook gently for 5 minutes to heat through. Garnish the soup with the croûtons and serve at once.

Serves 4-6.

POTAGE BONNE FEMME

60 g (2 oz/¼ cup) butter
500 g (1 lb) potatoes, diced
2 carrots, chopped
2 large leeks, trimmed and chopped
940 ml (1½ pints/3¾ cups) vegetable stock
salt and pepper
125 ml (4 fl oz/½ cup) double (thick) cream
1 tablespoon finely chopped fresh parsley or chervil

TO GARNISH: ½ carrot, cut into fine strips
½ small leek, cut into fine strips
1 slice bread, toasted

Melt butter in a saucepan and add prepared vegetables.

Cover and cook gently for 15 minutes. Add stock and bring to the boil, then re-cover and simmer for 20 minutes. Purée in a blender or food processor, then press through a sieve. Return soup to pan, add salt and pepper and stir in cream and parsley or chervil. Reheat very gently.

To make garnish, blanch the fine strips of carrot and leek in a pan for 1 minute, then drain. Cut out 4 small rounds of toast and divide the vegetables between them. Float on top of individual bowls of hot soup.

Serves 4.

— MINORCAN VEGETABLE SOUP —

2 red peppers (capsicums)
6 teaspoons olive oil
1 large Spanish onion
2 cloves garlic, finely chopped
250 g (8 oz) tomatoes, skinned, seeded and chopped
1 small cabbage
½ teaspoon dried thyme
1 bay leaf
1 teaspoon paprika
salt and pepper
4-6 thick slices bread, toasted
2 cloves garlic, halved

Place peppers (capsicums) under grill and turn until charred.

Put peppers (capsicums) into a polythene bag and leave for 15 minutes. Peel, cut off tops, remove seeds and chop. Heat oil in a large saucepan, add onion and cook until soft. Add peppers (capsicums), chopped garlic and tomatoes, then cover and cook gently for 15 minutes. Add 1.2 litres (2 pints/5 cups) water and bring to the boil.

Discard outside leaves from cabbage, then shred and add to soup with thyme, bay leaf and paprika and simmer for 15 minutes. Season with salt and pepper. Rub toast with a cut side of garlic. Lay a slice of toast in each soup plate, then ladle over the hot soup. Serve at once.

Serves 4-6.

— COURGETTE & TOMATO SOUP —

30 g (1 oz/6 teaspoons) butter
1 onion, finely chopped
375 g (12 oz) courgettes (zucchini), coarsely grated
1 clove garlic, crushed
625 ml (20 fl oz/2 ½ cups) vegetable stock
440 g (14 oz) can chopped tomatoes
2 tablespoons chopped fresh mixed herbs, if desired
salt and pepper
60 ml (2 fl oz/¼ cup) double (thick) cream and basil
   leaves, to garnish

Melt butter in a saucepan, add onion and cook until soft. Add courgettes (zucchini) and garlic and cook for 4-5 minutes.

Add stock and tomatoes with their juice, then bring to the boil, cover and simmer for 15 minutes.

Stir in herbs, if desired, and salt and pepper. Serve the soup in individual bowls, garnished with teaspoonfuls of cream stirred in or floating on the surface and basil leaves.

Serves 4.

CURRIED PARSNIP SOUP

45 g (1 ½ oz/9 teaspoons) butter
1 onion, chopped
1 teaspoon chopped fresh root ginger
1 teaspoon curry powder
½ teaspoon ground cumin
500 g (1 lb) parsnips, peeled and chopped
1 potato, chopped
940 ml (1 ½ pints/3 ¾ cups) beef stock
155 ml (5 fl oz/⅔ cup) plain yogurt
salt and pepper

CURRIED CROÛTONS: ½ teaspoon curry powder
squeeze lemon juice
30 g (1 oz/6 teaspoons) butter
2 thick slices bread

Melt butter in a saucepan, add onion and cook gently until soft. Stir in ginger, curry powder and cumin and cook for 1 minute, then add parsnips and potato and stir over a medium heat to coat vegetables with spicy butter. Pour in stock and bring to the boil, then cover and simmer for 30 minutes or until vegetables are very tender. Purée in a blender or food processor, then return to saucepan. Ladle a little soup into a bowl and whisk in yogurt, then pour back into pan.

Add salt and pepper and while reheating, make croûtons. Preheat oven to 200C (400F/ Gas 6). Beat curry powder, lemon juice and butter together in a bowl. Spread on bread, then remove crusts and cut into cubes. Place on a baking tray and bake until crisp and golden. Serve with soup.

Serves 4-6.

PISTOU

75 ml (2½ fl oz/⅓ cup) olive oil
1 onion, chopped
1 small potato, diced
2 carrots, sliced
2 sticks celery, finely sliced
bouquet garni
185 g (6 oz) French beans, cut into short lengths
2 small courgettes (zucchini), sliced
30 g (1 oz) broken spaghetti or pasta shapes
salt and pepper

PISTOU: 3 cloves garlic
4 tablespoons choppped fresh basil
60 g (2 oz/½ cup) freshly grated Parmesan cheese
2 tomatoes, skinned, seeded and chopped

Heat 3 teaspoons oil in a large saucepan, add onion and cook until just beginning to colour. Pour in 1.2 litres (2 pints/5 cups) water and bring to the boil. Add potato, carrots, celery and bouquet garni, and simmer for 10 minutes. Add beans, courgettes (zucchini) and pasta and simmer, uncovered, for 10-15 minutes, until tender.

Meanwhile, pound garlic and basil with a little salt in a mortar with a pestle. Gradually add cheese until it becomes a stiff paste, then add about one-third of the tomatoes. Continue to alternate the cheese and tomatoes, then slowly work in remaining olive oil to make a thick sauce. Remove and discard bouquet garni from soup. Season if necessary, then serve with pistou handed separately for each person to add to their bowl of soup, as desired.

Serves 4-6.

CREAM OF CAULIFLOWER SOUP

1 large cauliflower
salt and pepper
60 g (2 oz/¼ cup) butter
1 onion, chopped
30 g (1 oz/¼ cup) plain flour
500 ml (16 fl oz/2 cups) chicken stock
500 ml (16 fl oz/2 cups) milk
pinch grated nutmeg
60 ml (2 fl oz/¼ cup) crème fraîche

CHEESE SNIPPETS: 15 g (½ oz/6 teaspoons) freshly
   grated Parmesan cheese
45 g (1½ oz/9 teaspoons) butter
2 slices bread

Divide the cauliflower into tiny flowerets.

Plunge flowerets into boiling salted water for
3 minutes; drain. Melt butter in a saucepan,
add onion and cook until soft. Stir in flour,
and cook for 1 minute, then gradually stir in
stock. Bring to the boil, cover and simmer for
20 minutes. Strain into another pan, add
milk, cauliflower, salt and pepper and
nutmeg, then simmer for 10 minutes. With a
slotted spoon, remove one-third of the
cauliflower and reserve.

Purée remaining soup in a blender or food
processor, then return to pan and stir in
crème fraîche and reserved cauliflower.
Reheat very gently while making the
snippets. Preheat oven to 200C (400F/Gas
6). Beat cheese and butter together, spread
over bread, cut off crusts then cut into small
squares or diamonds. Bake until golden and
crisp. Serve soup garnished with cheese
snippets.

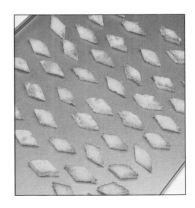

Serves 6.

— CREAM OF CARROT SOUP —

60 g (2 oz/¼ cup) butter
1 small onion, finely chopped
1 potato, diced
500 g (1 lb) carrots, chopped
750 ml (24 fl oz/3 cups) vegetable stock
pinch sugar
155 ml (5 fl oz/⅔ cup) single (light) cream
salt and pepper

HERBY CROÛTONS: 1 teaspoon dried mixed herbs
2 slices bread

Melt half the butter in a saucepan. Add onion, potato and carrots.

Cover and cook over low heat for 10 minutes. Add stock and sugar and bring to the boil, then cover and simmer for 30 minutes. Purée in a blender or food processor, then return to pan and add cream. Add salt and pepper.

To make croûtons, preheat oven to 200C (400F/Gas 6). Beat remaining butter and the mixed herbs together, then spread over bread. Cut into fancy shapes or squares and place on a baking tray. Bake until crisp and golden. Serve with the soup.

Serves 4.

PESTO SOUP

2 tablespoons olive oil
1 small onion, finely chopped
375 g (12 oz) courgettes (zucchini), diced
90 g (3 oz/½ cup) risotto rice
1.2 litres (2 pints/5 cups) hot chicken stock
salt and pepper

PESTO SAUCE: 30 g (1 oz) basil leaves
5 tablespoons olive oil
30 g (1 oz) pine nuts
2 cloves garlic
30 g (1 oz/¼ cup) freshly grated Parmesan cheese

PARMESAN CROÛTONS: 30 g (1 oz/6 teaspoons) butter
30 g (1 oz/¼ cup) freshly grated Parmesan cheese
2 slices bread

Heat oil in a large saucepan, add onion and courgettes (zucchini) and cook gently for 3-4 minutes, until soft. Stir in rice and coat the grains with oil. Pour in stock and bring to the boil, then simmer for 10 minutes, until rice is cooked. Season. Meanwhile, make pesto sauce. Put basil, olive oil, pine nuts, garlic and ¼ teaspoon salt into a blender or food processor and purée. Turn into a bowl and beat in the cheese.

To make croûtons, beat butter and cheese together. Toast bread on both sides, then spread with cheese butter and grill until melted and golden. Either cut out fancy shapes or remove crusts and dice. Stir 1 heaped tablespoon pesto sauce into soup before serving (store remainder in a jar in the refrigerator) and serve with cheese croûtons.

Serves 4-5.

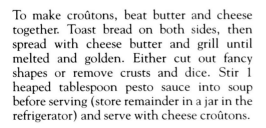

MINESTRONE

6 teaspoons olive oil
1 onion, chopped
1 clove garlic, crushed
1 small leek, trimmed and sliced
2 carrots, diced
2 sticks celery, sliced
1.9 litres (3 pints/7½ cups) chicken or beef stock
3 teaspoons tomato purée (paste)
440 g (14 oz) can haricot beans, drained
3 tomatoes, skinned, seeded and chopped
60 g (2 oz) French beans, cut into short lengths
185 g (6 oz) cabbage, shredded
30 g (1 oz) soup pasta
salt and pepper
2 tablespoons chopped fresh parsley
freshly grated Parmesan cheese, to garnish

Heat oil in a large saucepan, add onion, garlic and leek and cook over a low heat for 5 minutes. Add carrots, celery, stock, tomato purée (paste) and haricot beans, cover and simmer for 30 minutes. Stir in tomatoes and French beans and simmer for a further 10 minutes.

Stir in cabbage and pasta, add salt and pepper and cook for 10 minutes, until pasta is cooked. Stir in parsley and serve garnished with freshly grated Parmesan cheese.

Serves 6.

FRENCH TURNIP SOUP

30 g (1 oz/6 teaspoons) butter
500 g (1 lb) small white turnips, chopped
1 small onion, chopped
1.2 litres (2 pints/5 cups) vegetable stock
4 slices white bread, crusts removed
125 g (4 oz) shelled fresh peas
salt and pepper
pinch grated nutmeg

CHEESY PUFFS: 125 g (4 oz) puff pastry, thawed if frozen
45 g (1½ oz/9 teaspoons) cream cheese with herbs and
    garlic
1 egg, beaten, to glaze

Melt butter in a pan, add turnips and onion.

Cook gently for about 10 minutes, until they begin to soften. Add stock and bread and simmer gently for 25 minutes. Purée in a blender or food processor or sieve, then return to pan. Blanch peas for 2 minutes, then add to soup with salt and pepper and nutmeg.

To make garnish, preheat oven to 200C (400F/Gas 6). Roll out pastry thinly and cut into 5 cm (2 in) rounds. Place ½ teaspoon of cheese in each centre, dampen edges, fold over and place on a greased baking tray. Brush with beaten egg, then bake in the oven until crisp and golden. Float them on the hot soup when ready to serve.

Serves 4.

— CARROT & CORIANDER SOUP —

500 g (1 lb) carrots
6 teaspoons olive oil
1 small onion, finely chopped
1 clove garlic, crushed
1 teaspoon coriander seeds, crushed
1 teaspoon ground coriander
940 ml (1½ pints/3¾ cups) vegetable stock
60 g (2 oz/⅓ cup) sultanas, chopped
salt and pepper
1 tablespoon chopped fresh coriander leaves

SESAME CROÛTONS: 1 thick slice bread, crusts removed
15 g (½ oz/3 teaspoons) butter
3 teaspoons sesame seeds

Cut 2 carrots into small dice and set aside. Chop remaining carrots. Heat oil in a large saucepan, add onion, garlic and chopped carrots and cook gently for 10 minutes. Stir in crushed and ground coriander and cook for 1 minute. Add 750 ml (24 fl oz/3 cups) of the stock, cover and simmer for 15 minutes, or until the carrots are tender. Meanwhile, put diced carrots in a small saucepan with remaining stock and simmer until tender.

Purée soup in a blender or food processor, then return to pan. Add diced carrots, sultanas and salt and pepper. Reheat gently while making the croûtons. Toast bread on each side until golden. Cool, then spread with butter and sprinkle over sesame seeds. Return to grill until golden. Cut into small cubes. To serve, stir in chopped coriander and garnish with sesame seed croûtons.

Serves 4.

GARLIC SOUP

45 g (1 ½ oz/9 teaspoons) butter
6 cloves garlic
30 g (1 oz/¼ cup) plain flour
625 ml (20 fl oz/2 ½ cups) chicken stock
155 ml (5 fl oz/⅔ cup) dry white wine
1 teaspoon dried thyme
salt and pepper
1 egg yolk
155 ml (5 fl oz/⅔ cup) single (light) cream
90 g (3 oz/¾ cup) ground almonds
green grapes, to garnish

Melt butter in a saucepan, slightly crush
garlic, add to pan and cook for 3-4 minutes,
or until golden.

Stir in flour and cook for 1 minute, then
gradually stir in stock. Add wine, thyme, salt
and pepper and simmer for 10 minutes. Beat
egg yolk and cream together in a large bowl,
then strain soup into bowl, whisking
constantly.

Return to rinsed-out pan and stir in almonds.
Reheat gently: do not boil. Halve and remove
pips from grapes and use to garnish soup.

Serves 4.

– HUNGARIAN CABBAGE SOUP –

6 teaspoons vegetable oil
375 g (12 oz) red cabbage, finely shredded
1 onion, finely sliced
1 clove garlic, crushed
½ teaspoon caraway seeds
440 g (14 oz) can sieved tomatoes
3 teaspoons red wine vinegar
940 ml (1½ pints/3¼ cups) chicken or veal stock
salt and pepper
90 ml (3 fl oz/⅓ cup) thick sour cream and 1
    tablespoon chopped fresh dill, to garnish

Put oil in a large saucepan and add cabbage
and onion.

Cover and cook over medium heat for about
20 minutes, until cabbage has softened. Add
remaining ingredients except pepper and
garnish, then cover and gently simmer for 30
minutes.

To serve, season with pepper. Stir dill into
sour cream, then spoon on top of individual
portions of soup.

Serves 4-6.

— WINTER VEGETABLE BROTH —

30 g (1 oz/6 teaspoons) butter
1 onion, sliced
250 g (8 oz) carrots, diced
250 g (8 oz) swede, diced
1 potato, diced
2 large parsnips, diced
500 ml (16 fl oz/2 cups) vegetable stock
1 bay leaf
3 teaspoons cornflour
500 ml (16 fl oz/2 cups) milk
salt and pepper
90 g (3 oz) frozen peas
2 small bread rolls and 60 g (2 oz/½ cup) Cheddar
    cheese, grated, to garnish

Melt butter in a saucepan, add vegetables, except peas, cover and cook gently for 10 minutes. Add stock and bay leaf, re-cover and simmer for 30 minutes. Blend cornflour with a little milk, then add to soup with remaining milk and cook, stirring until thickened. Remove bay leaf and add salt and pepper.

Stir peas into soup and simmer for 2-3 minutes while making garnish. Cut bread rolls in half, divide the cheese between them and grill until melted. Place on top of each portion of soup just before serving.

Serves 4.

CLEAR VEGETABLE SOUP

2 young carrots, thinly sliced
2 sticks celery, sliced
60 g (2 oz) button mushrooms, sliced
125 g (4 oz) broccoli flowerets
45 g (1½ oz) frozen peas
1 courgette (zucchini), cut into thin strips

VEGETABLE STOCK: 1 small onion, thinly sliced
1 leek, chopped
2 sticks celery, chopped
3 carrots, chopped
2 tomatoes, chopped
bouquet garni
2 bay leaves
salt
½ teaspoon black peppercorns

To make stock, put all ingredients into a saucepan, add 1.2 litres (2 pints/5 cups) water. Bring to the boil and simmer for 40 minutes, then strain; this stock does not need degreasing. For a stronger flavour, boil rapidly for 5 minutes to reduce to 940 ml (1½ pints/ 3¾ cups). Put the stock into rinsed-out pan, add sliced carrots, celery, mushrooms and broccoli. Bring to the boil, cover and simmer for 5 minutes.

Stir in peas and courgettes (zucchini) and cook for a further 2 minutes. Season to taste before serving.

Serves 4.

── GOLDEN VEGETABLE SOUP ──

375 g (12 oz) carrots, chopped
250 g (8 oz) swede, chopped
2 small leeks, trimmed and chopped
125 g (4 oz) potatoes, diced
940 ml (1½ pints/3¾ cups) vegetable stock
315 ml (10 fl oz/1¼ cups) milk
salt and pepper
90 ml (3 fl oz/⅓ cup) double (thick) cream and 1
**   tablespoon chopped fresh parsley, to garnish**

Put all the vegetables in a large saucepan, add
stock and bring to the boil. Cover and simmer
for 30 minutes, until tender.

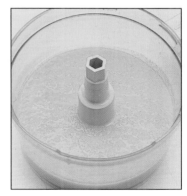

Purée in a blender or food processor, then
return to rinsed-out pan and stir in milk.
Reheat and add salt and pepper.

When ready to serve, whip cream until
holding its shape and stir in parsley. Float a
spoonful of herb chantilly on each portion
and serve at once.

Serves 4-6.

— CREAM OF MUSHROOM SOUP —

60 g (2 oz/¼ cup) butter
375 g (12 oz) mushrooms, finely chopped
60 g (2 oz/½ cup) plain flour
500 ml (16 fl oz/2 cups) chicken stock
155 ml (5 fl oz/⅔ cup) milk
1 tablespoon chopped fresh parsley
3 teaspoons lemon juice
salt and pepper
155 ml (5 fl oz/⅔ cup) single (light) cream
75 ml (2½ fl oz/⅓ cup) double (thick) cream and 1
   tablespoon finely chopped fresh watercress, to
   garnish

Melt the butter in a large saucepan, add
mushrooms and cook gently for 5 minutes.

Stir in flour and cook for 1 minute, then
gradually add stock and milk. Bring to the
boil, then cover and simmer for 10 minutes.
Add parsley, lemon juice and salt and pepper,
then stir in single (light) cream and reheat
gently.

When ready to serve, whip double (thick)
cream until holding its shape and stir in
watercress. Float a spoonful of the watercress
chantilly on each portion, and serve at once.

Serves 4.

SOUP GEORGETTE

30 g (1 oz/6 teaspoons) butter
1 onion, chopped
250 g (8 oz) carrots, chopped
250 g (8 oz) leeks, trimmed and chopped
500 g (1 lb) tomatoes, skinned and chopped
750 ml (24 fl oz/3 cups) chicken stock
small rosemary sprig
salt and pepper
90 ml (3 fl oz/⅓ cup) single (light) cream
2 tomatoes and rosemary sprigs, to garnish

Melt the butter in a saucepan, add onion, carrots and leeks and cook for 5 minutes. Stir in tomatoes and cook for 5 minutes.

Add stock to the pan with rosemary sprig, bring to the boil, then cover and simmer for 35 minutes. Discard rosemary and purée the soup in a blender or food processor, then return to pan. Season with salt and pepper and stir in cream.

Skin and discard seeds from the 2 tomatoes, then chop. Serve soup garnished with freshly chopped tomatoes and rosemary sprigs.

Serves 6.

FRENCH ONION SOUP

30 g (1 oz/6 teaspoons) butter
6 teaspoons olive oil
500 g (1 lb) onions, thinly sliced
pinch caster sugar
1.2 litres (2 pints/5 cups) beef stock
1 bay leaf
salt and pepper

TO GARNISH: 4 thick slices French stick
1 teaspoon Dijon mustard
90 g (3 oz/¾ cup) Gruyère cheese, grated

Heat butter and oil together in a large saucepan. Add onions and sugar.

Cook over medium heat for about 20 minutes, stirring occasionally, until onions are deep golden brown. Add stock and bay leaf and slowly bring to the boil, then cover and simmer for 25 minutes. Remove bay leaf and add salt and pepper.

To make garnish, toast bread on each side, then spread with a little mustard. Ladle soup into 4 flameproof bowls and float a slice of bread in each. Pile cheese on to each slice and place bowls under a hot grill until cheese has melted and is bubbling. Serve at once.

Serves 4.

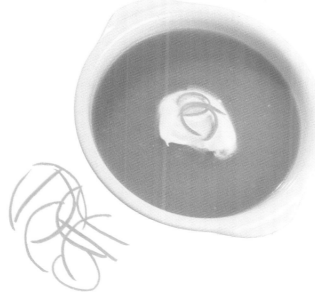

— TOMATO & ORANGE SOUP —

1 orange
3 teaspoons sunflower oil
1 small onion, chopped
1 clove garlic, crushed
750 g (1½ lb) ripe tomatoes, coarsely chopped
500 ml (16 fl oz/2 cups) chicken stock
1 teaspoon sugar
1 teaspoon chopped fresh basil
salt and pepper
60 ml (2 fl oz/¼ cup) double (thick) cream, whipped

Using a potato peeler, cut 4 strips of peel from orange and reserve for garnish. Grate remaining peel and squeeze the juice.

Heat oil in a saucepan, add onion and garlic and cook over low heat for 5 minutes until soft. Add tomatoes and grated peel and cook over medium heat for 5 minutes, until tomatoes become soft. Pour in stock and add sugar and basil, cover and simmer for 15 minutes.

Meanwhile, cut reserved orange peel into thin strips and drop into a pan of simmering water for 3 minutes, then drain and spread on a piece of absorbent kitchen paper. Purée soup in a blender or food processor, then press through a sieve. Return to pan and add salt and pepper. Stir in orange juice and reheat gently. Serve with a spoonful of whipped cream in each bowl, topped with a few shreds of orange peel.

Serves 4.

FLORENTINE SOUP

750 g (1 ½ lb) spinach
60 g (2 oz/¼ cup) butter
1 shallot, chopped
30 g (1 oz/¼ cup) plain flour
500 ml (16 fl oz/2 cups) chicken or vegetable stock
salt and pepper
¼ teaspoon grated nutmeg
500 ml (16 fl oz/2 cups) milk
105 ml (3 ½ fl oz/⅓ cup) double (thick) cream
2 very small hard-boiled eggs, sliced, to garnish

Pick over spinach, discarding stalks, and wash thoroughly.

Put spinach into a large saucepan and cook over medium heat until tender. Turn into a colander and press out as much water as possible. Melt butter in a large saucepan, add shallot, and cook until soft. Stir in flour and cook for 1 minute, then add stock and spinach, cover and simmer for 15 minutes. Season with salt and pepper and nutmeg.

Purée in a blender or food processor or sieve, then return to pan, add milk and reheat gently. Just before serving, stir in 45 ml (1½ fl oz/9 teaspoons) cream. To serve, swirl remaining cream on each portion and garnish with hard-boiled egg slices.

Serves 4.

HOT & SOUR SOUP

1.2 litres (2 pints/5 cups) chicken stock
9 teaspoons rice vinegar
3 teaspoons dry sherry
2 teaspoons soy sauce
1 small clove garlic, finely chopped
½ teaspoon finely chopped fresh root ginger
5 dried Chinese mushrooms, covered with hot water
    and soaked for 20 minutes
1 carrot, cut into thin strips
90 g (3 oz) canned bamboo shoots, rinsed and cut into
    thin strips
½ teaspoon Tabasco or chilli sauce
6 teaspoons cornflour
125 g (4 oz) tofu, cut into strips
2 spring onions, shredded

Put the stock into a saucepan and bring to the boil, then add rice vinegar, sherry, soy sauce, garlic and ginger. Drain mushrooms, remove stems, slice and add to pan with carrot, bamboo shoots and Tabasco or chilli sauce. Bring to the boil, then simmer for 10 minutes.

Blend cornflour with 9 teaspoons water, and stir into soup with tofu, then simmer for 2 minutes to thicken. Scatter over spring onions and serve at once.

Serves 6.

CELERY & ONION SOUP

1 head celery
2 onions
60 (2 oz/¼ cup) butter
3 teaspoons plain flour
750 ml (24 fl oz/3 cups) milk
1 bay leaf
60 ml (2 fl oz/¼ cup) crème fraîche
salt and pepper

Take 1 stick of celery and cut into thin strips, place in a bowl of iced water and set aside. Reserve a few leaves for garnish. Reserve one quarter of an onion, then chop remaining onion and celery.

Melt butter in a saucepan, add onion and celery and cook for 5 minutes. Stir in flour and cook for 1 minute, then gradually stir in milk. Add bay leaf, cover and simmer for 20 minutes.

Cool slightly, remove bay leaf, then purée soup in a blender or food processor. Return to pan, stir in crème fraîche and add salt and pepper. Reheat gently. Chop reserved onion and add to soup. Drain celery curls and use to garnish soup with reserved leaves.

Serves 4-6.

BORSCHT

1 onion
2 large carrots
2 sticks celery
500 g (1 lb) beetroot
1.5 litres (2½ pints/6 cups) strong beef stock
2 cloves garlic
3 teaspoons soft brown sugar
6 teaspoons red wine vinegar
1 bay leaf
1 teaspoon caraway seeds
salt and pepper
125 g (4 oz) white cabbage, shredded
155 ml (5 fl oz/⅔ cup) thick sour cream
250 g (8 oz) boiled potatoes, diced
6 teaspoons chopped fresh parsley

Cut onion, carrots, celery and beetroot into matchstick strips. Bring stock to the boil and add vegetables, garlic, sugar, vinegar, bay leaf and caraway seeds. Add salt and return to the boil, then cover and simmer for 20 minutes.

Stir in cabbage and cook for a further 20 minutes until all vegetables are tender. Season with pepper and salt again if necessary. To serve, ladle the soup into warm bowls. Top with sour cream and add diced potato, then scatter over parsley.

Serves 6.

RICH COUNTRY CHICKEN SOUP

45 g (1½ oz/9 teaspoons) butter
125 g (4 oz) button mushrooms, chopped
45 g (1½ oz/⅓ cup) plain flour
625 ml (20 fl oz/2½ cups) strong chicken stock
625 ml (20 fl oz/2½ cups) milk
375 g (12 oz) cooked skinless chicken, diced
2 egg yolks
155 ml (5 fl oz/⅔ cup) single (thin) cream
salt and pepper

WATERCRESS DUMPLINGS: 125 g (4 oz/1 cup) self-raising
    flour
pinch dried mixed herbs
60 g (2 oz) shredded suet
1 bunch watercress, trimmed and finely chopped
1 small egg, beaten

Melt butter in a saucepan, add mushrooms and cook gently for 4-5 minutes. Stir in flour, and cook for 1 minute, then gradually add stock and milk. Bring to the boil, stirring constantly, then cover and simmer for 15 minutes. Meanwhile, make dumplings. Sift flour into a bowl, then mix in ½ teaspoon salt, herbs, suet and watercress. Add egg and 3 teaspoons water and mix to a soft dough. Divide into 24 pieces and roll into balls. Bring a pan of water to the boil, drop dumplings into the simmering liquid, cover and simmer for 10 minutes.

Take soup off heat and stir in chicken. Beat egg yolks and cream together, ladle in a little soup and mix quickly, then pour back into pan and heat gently until thickens: do not boil. Add salt and pepper if necessary. Lift dumplings out of water with a slotted spoon and add to the soup just before serving.

Serves 6.

Note: For extra flavour, cook the dumplings in stock instead of water.

—— CHICKEN NOODLE SOUP ——

60 g (2 oz) fine-cut vermicelli
1 tablespoon finely chopped fresh parsley

CHICKEN STOCK: 1 chicken carcass, raw or cooked, to
    include giblets but not liver
1 small onion, sliced
1 large carrot, sliced
1 stick celery, chopped
2-3 fresh parsley stalks
1 teaspoon salt
6 black peppercorns

To make stock, put chicken carcass into a
large pan, cover with water and bring to the
boil.

Skim off any scum that rises to surface. Add
remaining stock ingredients and simmer
gently 2½-3 hours, skimming as necessary.
Strain and cool, then refrigerate overnight.
Next day, remove any fat from surface.
Measure 940 ml (1½ pints/3¾ cups) stock
into a pan and reheat, seasoning if necessary.

Bring a pan of salted water to the boil,
crumble in vermicelli and simmer for 4-5
minutes. Drain and rinse, then place in a
soup tureen and pour over soup. Sprinkle
with parsley before serving.

Serves 4.

SCOTCH BROTH

1 kg (2 lb) neck of lamb, cut into pieces
1.5 litres (2½ pints/6 cups) light stock
60 g (2 oz/¼ cup) pearl barley
salt and pepper
1 large onion, chopped
2 leeks, trimmed and chopped
2 sticks celery, chopped
1 small turnip, diced
1 large carrot, sliced
bouquet garni
1 tablespoon chopped fresh parsley, to garnish

Put lamb into a large saucepan with stock and slowly bring to the boil. Skim off any scum that rises to surface.

Add barley and salt and pepper, cover and simmer for 2 hours. Lift out lamb and take meat off bones. Discard fat, then return meat to pan.

Add remaining ingredients except parsley to soup and bring back to simmering point. Cover and cook for 30 minutes, or until the vegetables are tender. Discard bouquet garni, season if necessary and serve garnished with chopped parsley.

Serves 6.

MULLIGATAWNY

500 g (1 lb) piece shin of beef
5 cm (2 in) piece fresh root ginger, peeled
2 bay leaves
1 onion, chopped
1 teaspoon turmeric
½ teaspoon chilli powder
2 teaspoons coriander seeds, crushed
2 teaspoons cumin seeds, crushed
8 black peppercorns, crushed
1 small cooking apple, peeled, cored and chopped
1 carrot, sliced
30 g (1 oz/2 tablespoons) red lentils, rinsed
2 cloves garlic, chopped
salt
3 teaspoons lemon juice

Put beef into a large saucepan, pour in 1.9 litres (3 pints/7½ cups) water and bring to the boil. Skim surface, then add all remaining ingredients except lemon juice. Cover and simmer very gently for 2½-3 hours, until the beef is tender. Remove beef from the pan and set aside. Sieve soup into a bowl, rubbing vegetables through; discard pulp. Cool, then chill both the meat and stock.

To serve, remove solidified fat from surface of soup, then put into a pan and reheat. Cut beef into small pieces, add to soup with lemon juice and salt if necessary. Simmer for 5 minutes.

Serves 6.

Note: Serve the soup with fried croûtons, see page 102, adding 3 crushed garlic cloves to the oil.

COCK-A-LEEKIE

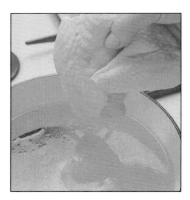

2 large chicken joints
1.2 litres (2 pints/5 cups) chicken stock
bouquet garni
4 leeks
12 prunes, soaked for 1 hour and drained
salt and pepper

OATY DUMPLINGS: 125 g (4 oz/¾ cup) porridge oats
60 g (2 oz/1 cup) fresh wholemeal breadcrumbs
1 tablespoon chopped fresh herbs
60 g (2 oz/¼ cup) margarine

Put chicken joints into a saucepan with stock
and bouquet garni.

Bring to the boil, then cover and simmer for
30 minutes. Remove chicken from pan and
leave to cool. Discard bouquet garni and skim
off any fat from surface of soup. Trim coarse
outer leaves from leeks, then split
lengthwise. Wash well, then cut into 2.5 cm
(1 in) pieces. Add to soup with prunes and
simmer for 25 minutes. Cut chicken meat
into small pieces and return to soup. Add salt
and pepper.

To make dumplings, put oats and
breadcrumbs into a bowl and stir in herbs,
and salt and pepper. Rub in margarine, then
add 6-9 teaspoons cold water and mix to a
dough. Divide into small balls, then drop
into soup, cover and simmer for 15 minutes,
until dumplings are cooked.

Serves 6.

— DEVILLED TURKEY SOUP —

3 teaspoons vegetable oil
1 onion, chopped
2 teaspoons curry powder
½ teaspoon mustard powder
375 g (12 oz) potatoes, diced
940 ml (1½ pints/3¾ cups) chicken stock
2 teaspoons Worcestershire sauce
185 g (6 oz) cooked turkey meat, diced
salt and pepper

LEMON DUMPLINGS: 125 g (4 oz/1 cup) self-raising
   wholemeal flour
60 g (2 oz/¼ cup) sunflower margarine
grated peel and juice of ½ lemon

Heat oil in a saucepan, add onion and cook gently until soft. Stir in curry and mustard powders and cook for 1 minute. Add potatoes and stock, bring to the boil, cover and simmer for 30 minutes. Add Worcestershire sauce, turkey and salt and pepper and slowly bring back to simmering point.

To make dumplings, put flour into a bowl with a good pinch of salt and rub in the margarine. Add lemon peel and juice and mix to a soft dough. Roll into small balls, then drop into the soup, cover and cook for 5 minutes, until doubled in size. Serve at once.

Serves 4.

—— GERMAN SAUSAGE SOUP ——

1 large potato, diced
1 large onion, sliced
3 sticks celery, chopped
440 g (14 oz) can chopped tomatoes
940 ml (1½ pints/3¾ cups) beef or ham stock
½ teaspoon caraway seeds
250 g (8 oz) can red kidney beans, drained and rinsed
125 g (4 oz) cabbage, shredded
125 g (4 oz) frankfurters, thickly sliced
125 g (4 oz) piece German sausage, such as bierwurst
  or ham sausage, diced
salt and pepper

Put potato, onion, celery, tomatoes, stock and caraway seeds into a large pan.

Bring to the boil, cover and simmer for 20 minutes. Add beans and cabbage and simmer for a further 20 minutes, until tender.

Stir in frankfurters, sausage and salt and pepper, then cook for a few minutes to heat through.

Serves 4-6.

OXTAIL SOUP

1 oxtail, cut into pieces
9 teaspoons vegetable oil
2 sticks celery, chopped
2 carrots, chopped
2 small onions, sliced
155 ml (5 fl oz/⅔ cup) dry red wine
bouquet garni
6 black peppercorns, slightly crushed
salt and pepper
½ teaspoon dried thyme
4 cloves
4 teaspoons arrowroot
¼ teaspoon cayenne
Watercress Dumplings, see page 84

Wash oxtail and trim off fat. Heat oil in a large saucepan, add oxtail and fry until browned. Transfer to a plate. Add vegetables and cook until beginning to brown. Add oxtail and 1.5 litres (2½ pints/6 cups) water, wine, bouquet garni, peppercorns, salt, thyme and cloves. Bring to the boil, skimming. Cover and slowly simmer for 3 hours. Lift oxtail from soup and set aside. Remove meat from bones, discarding gristle. Strain soup into a bowl and add pieces of oxtail meat. Skim off any fat.

Make the dumplings. Reheat soup, blend arrowroot with a little water and stir into the soup with the cayenne and salt and pepper. When soup reaches simmering point, drop in the dumplings, cover and simmer for 10 minutes. Serve when the dumplings are cooked.

Serves 6.

Variation: Substitute parsley for the watercress in the dumplings, if preferred.

BEEF & PASTA SOUP

185 g (6 oz) capellini (very fine spaghetti)

BEEF STOCK: 500 g (1 lb) shin of beef, cut into pieces
500 g (1 lb) marrow bones or knuckle of veal
1 onion, sliced
1 large carrot, sliced
bouquet garni
1 teaspoon salt
5 black peppercorns
1 bay leaf

PARMESAN BALLS: 30 g (1 oz/¼ cup) freshly grated
    Parmesan cheese
2 egg yolks

Preheat oven to 220C (425F/Gas 7). Put meat and bones in a roasting tin and roast for 15 minutes to brown, then turn meat and bones over and cook for a further 10 minutes. Transfer to a saucepan, add 1.8 litres (3 pints/ 7½ cups) water and bring to boil, skimming the surface. When only white foam is left, add onion, carrot, bouquet garni, salt, peppercorns and bay leaf. Cover and simmer very gently for 3 hours. (This should yield 1.2 litres (2 pints/5 cups) stock.)

Strain stock, cool and refrigerate. Next day, remove fat from surface and return stock to a pan. Reheat, seasoning if necessary. When simmering point is reached, break up pasta, drop into soup and cook for about 6 minutes, until just tender. To make Parmesan balls, mix cheese and egg yolks together, then drop ½ teaspoons of mixture over surface of soup. Cover and cook for about 4 minutes, until pasta is cooked. Serve at once.

Serves 6.

GOULASH SOUP

6 teaspoons vegetable oil
500 g (1 lb) lean stewing meat, cut into 0.5 cm (¼ in)
  cubes
1 large onion, thinly sliced
1 clove garlic, crushed
½ teaspoon ground cumin
2 teaspoons paprika
3 teaspoons plain flour
1.2 litres (2 pints/5 cups) beef stock
1 large potato
440 g (14 oz) can chopped tomatoes
salt and pepper
thick sour cream and paprika, to garnish

Heat oil in a large saucepan; add beef cubes
and onion.

Cook over medium heat for 4-6 minutes until
meat is browned and onion soft. Stir in garlic,
cumin, paprika and flour and cook for 1
minute. Gradually add stock and bring to the
boil, then cover and simmer for 2 hours.

Dice potato and add to soup with tomatoes
and their juice and salt and pepper. Continue
cooking for 30 minutes, until potatoes are
tender. Serve garnished with spoonfuls of
sour cream, sprinkled with paprika.

Serves 6.

HARIRA

6 teaspoons vegetable oil
375 g (12 oz) lean lamb, cut into small cubes
1 onion, sliced
2 teaspoons ground coriander
½ teaspoon ground turmeric
½ teaspoon cayenne
½ teaspoon ground ginger
½ teaspoon ground cumin
250 g (8 oz) tomatoes, peeled and chopped
1 clove garlic, crushed
440 g (14 oz) can chick peas, drained and rinsed
salt and pepper
juice of 1 lemon or 2 limes
1 tablespoon chopped fresh coriander
¼ teaspoon ground cinnamon, to garnish

Heat oil in a large saucepan, add cubes of lamb and fry quickly until they are evenly browned all over. Reduce heat, add onion and cook for 5 minutes, stirring constantly. Stir in all spices, except cinnamon for garnish, and cook for 1 minute, then add tomatoes, garlic and 625 ml (20 fl oz/2½ cups) water.

Mash three-quarters of the chick peas, add to soup with whole chick peas and salt and pepper. Bring to the boil, cover and simmer for 40 minutes, or until the meat is tender. Just before serving, stir in lemon or lime juice and coriander and simmer for a further 2 minutes. Serve soup sprinkled with cinnamon.

Serves 4-6.

— PHEASANT & LENTIL SOUP —

1 small pheasant, cleaned
1 onion, thickly sliced
1 large carrot, thickly sliced
2 sticks celery, chopped
1 bay leaf
thyme sprig
8 black peppercorns
125 g (4 oz/²⁄₃ cup) continental brown lentils, rinsed
2 small leeks, trimmed and chopped
salt and pepper

Put pheasant into a large saucepan with 1.9 litres (3 pints/7½ cups) water. Bring slowly to the boil, skimming off any scum which rises to the surface.

Add onion, carrot, celery, bay leaf, thyme and peppercorns, cover and simmer for 45 minutes. Lift out pheasant, and when cool enough to handle remove breast meat. Return carcass to pan and cook for a further 2 hours. Strain stock and when cool, place in the refrigerator with the reserved breast meat and best bits of leg meat. Leave overnight. Next day, remove fat from soup. Measure soup and return to pan. Bring to the boil, reduce to 1.5 litres (2½ pints/6 cups) by simmering, or make up with water if not enough.

Add lentils and leeks to pan, cover and simmer for 45 minutes, or until lentils are tender. Meanwhile, dice reserved meat. Add to soup with salt and pepper and simmer a few minutes to heat through.

Serves 6.

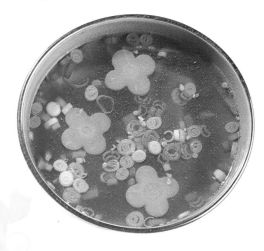

ORIENTAL CHICKEN SOUP

1 clove garlic, finely chopped
1 piece lemon grass, halved lengthwise
1 carrot, cut into flowers
2 spring onions, chopped
60 g (2 oz) cooked chicken breast (fillet), shredded
60 g (2 oz) mange tout (snow peas), cut into strips

CHICKEN CONSOMMÉ: 125 g (4 oz) minced veal
1 carrot, finely chopped
1 stick celery, finely chopped
1 leek, trimmed, and finely sliced
1 thyme sprig and 1 bay leaf
1.8 litres (3 pints/7½ cups) chicken stock
salt and pepper
2 egg whites

To make consommé, put veal, vegetables, herbs and stock into a large saucepan with salt and pepper and begin to heat. Whisk egg whites and pour into pan, whisking constantly until a thick froth starts to form. When boiling, stop whisking and lower heat to maintain a very slow simmer: do not boil. Simmer, covered, for 1 hour. Line a large sieve or colander with muslin and stand it over a bowl. Draw scum back from surface of consommé.

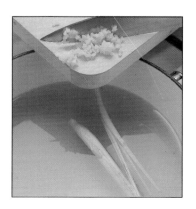

Ladle clarified stock into the muslin-lined sieve. Place a piece of absorbent kitchen paper over surface to absorb any fat. Measure 940 ml (1½ pints/3¾ cups) consommé into a pan, add garlic and lemon grass and simmer for 15 minutes. Meanwhile, blanch carrot flowers for 2 minutes. Remove lemon grass and add spring onions, chicken and mange tout (snow peas) and simmer for 2 minutes. Add carrot flowers just before serving.

Serves 4.

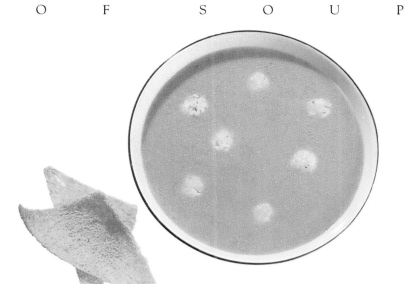

CHICKEN LIVER SOUP

125 g (4 oz) chicken livers, thawed if frozen
30 g (1 oz/6 teaspoons) butter
1 shallot, finely chopped
30 g (1 oz/¼ cup) plain flour
625 ml (20 fl oz/2½ cups) chicken stock
salt and pepper
9 teaspoons dry sherry

EGG BALLS: 2 eggs, hard-boiled
1 egg yolk
1 teaspoon chopped fresh parsley
30 g (1 oz/½ cup) fresh breadcrumbs
15 g (½ oz/2 tablespoons) ground almonds
flour for rolling

Clean chicken livers, cutting away any green parts. Melt butter in a saucepan, add shallot and cook gently until soft. Add livers and cook for 1 minute. Stir in flour and cook for a further minute, then gradually stir in stock and salt and pepper and simmer for 3-4 minutes. Sieve soup and return to the pan. Add sherry and more seasoning if necessary.

To make egg balls, rub hard-boiled eggs through a sieve, and mix with remaining ingredients, adding salt and pepper to taste, to make a stiff paste. With floured hands, roll into tiny balls. Drop into a pan of salted simmering water and cook for 5 minutes. Reheat soup without boiling, then lift out egg balls with a slotted spoon and transfer them to soup. Serve at once.

Serves 4.

ITALIAN BEEFBALL SOUP

1 large carrot, cut into thick matchstick strips
1 leek, trimmed and shredded
1 small turnip, cut into thick matchstick strips
15 g (½ oz/3 teaspoons) butter
940 ml (1½ pints/3¾ cups) Beef Consommé, see page 108

MEATBALLS: 185 g (6 oz) very lean minced beef
1 small egg
1 teaspoon finely chopped onion
3 teaspoons fresh breadcrumbs
2 teaspoons chopped fresh parsley
pinch grated nutmeg
salt and pepper

To make meatballs, put minced beef into a food processor and work until finely chopped or press through a mincer. Transfer to a bowl and mix in remaining ingredients. With damp hands, roll into 16 small balls the size of a walnut. Bring a pan of water to the boil, lower to simmering point and drop in meatballs. Cook gently for 10 minutes. Lift out with a slotted spoon and set aside.

Put prepared vegetables into a saucepan with butter and 155 ml (5 fl oz/⅔ cup) of the consommé. Cover and cook over medium heat for 5 minutes. Add remaining consommé and meatballs and bring to the boil, then simmer 2-3 minutes, until meatballs are reheated. Add salt and pepper if necessary.

Serves 4.

— CHICKEN & KNEIDLACH SOUP —

1 large chicken breast (fillet) portion
1 onion, chopped
1 large carrot, chopped
1.2 litres (2 pints/5 cups) chicken stock
chervil leaves, to garnish

KNEIDLACH (DUMPLINGS): 6 teaspoons oil
1 small onion, finely chopped
60 g (2 oz/½ cup) medium matzo meal
salt and pepper
3 teaspoons ground almonds
1 egg, beaten

Put chicken, onion, carrot and stock into a large saucepan with salt and pepper and bring to the boil. Cover and simmer for 1 hour. Meanwhile, make mixture for kneidlach. Heat oil in a small frying pan, add onion and sauté until soft. Strain oil into a bowl and discard onion. Add matzo meal to bowl with salt and pepper, ground almonds, egg and 125 ml (4 fl oz/½ cup) boiling water. Mix well to make a soft dough, then cover and refrigerate for 30 minutes.

Remove chicken from soup and strain soup into another pan. Cut chicken into small pieces and return to soup. To cook kneidlach, roll mixture into 12 small balls with damp hands. Bring a pan of water to simmering point and drop balls into water. Simmer, covered, for 6-8 minutes, until doubled in size. Lift out with a slotted spoon and transfer to soup. Serve garnished with chervil leaves.

Serves 6.

ICED MELON SOUP

2 different coloured melons, weighing about 750 g (1½
  lb) each, such as galia, cantaloupe, honeydew
knob fresh root ginger, peeled
125 g (4 oz/½ cup) sugar
250 ml (8 fl oz/1 cup) dry white wine

Cut each melon in half and discard pips.
Scoop out a few small balls from the green
(galia) melon and set aside. Scoop out the
remaining flesh from melons, keeping both
varieties separate.

Put 625 ml (20 fl oz/2½ cups) water in a
saucepan with ginger and sugar and simmer
for 5 minutes. Cool, then remove ginger. Put
half of the wine into a blender or food
processor with one variety of melon flesh and
pour in half the cooled syrup. Blend, then
pour into a bowl. Repeat with remaining
wine and syrup and other melon flesh.

Chill both bowls of soup for at least 1 hour. To
serve, pour green-coloured soup (galia) into
individual bowls, then pour orange-coloured
soup (cantaloupe) in the middle. Garnish
with reserved melon balls.

Serves 4-6.

SUMMER TOMATO BISQUE

1 kg (2 lb) ripe tomatoes, chopped
3 spring onions, chopped
½ red pepper (capsicum), seeded and chopped
2 cloves garlic, crushed
500 ml (16 fl oz/2 cups) vegetable stock
1 teaspoon sugar
2 tablespoons chopped fresh basil
60 ml (2 fl oz/¼ cup) crème fraîche or natural yogurt
salt and pepper
1 avocado and snipped fresh chives, to garnish

Put tomatoes, spring onions, red pepper (capsicum) and garlic in a saucepan with stock and sugar.

Bring to the boil, then cover and simmer for 15 minutes. Remove from heat and leave to cool. Purée in a blender or food processor, then sieve into a bowl. Cover and chill for 2 hours. Stir in the basil, crème fraîche or yogurt and add salt and pepper.

Halve avocado and discard stone, peel and slice. Ladle soup into individual bowls, arrange avocado slices on top, then sprinkle with snipped chives and serve.

Serves 6.

MANGE TOUT SOUP

30 g (1 oz/6 teaspoons) butter
5 spring onions, chopped
375 g (12 oz) mange tout (snow peas), trimmed
625 ml (20 fl oz/2½ cups) chicken stock
½ small lettuce, shredded
1 teaspoon sugar
1 tablespoon chopped fresh mint
155 ml (5 fl oz/⅔ cup) crème fraîche
salt and pepper

CROÛTONS: 2 slices bread
vegetable oil for frying

Melt butter in a saucepan, add spring onions and cook gently for 3-4 minutes.

Reserve 6 mange tout (snow peas), then chop remainder and add to pan with stock, lettuce and sugar and simmer for 5 minutes. Purée in a blender or food processor, then sieve and return to pan. Add mint, stir in crème fraîche and salt and pepper and reheat gently: do not boil. Do not reheat too long or the soup will loose its fresh colour.

Shred the reserved mange tout (snow peas) and blanch for 30 seconds, then drain. Cut bread into fancy shapes and fry in oil until crisp and golden. Drain on absorbent kitchen paper. Garnish the soup with the shreds of mange tout (snow peas) and croûtons.

Serves 4.

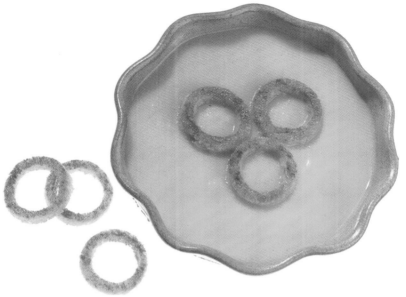

PUMPKIN SOUP

1.5 kg (3 lb) pumpkin
30 g (1 oz/6 teaspoons) butter
1 onion, chopped
625 ml (20 fl oz/2½ cups) chicken stock
1 teaspoon light brown sugar
good pinch grated nutmeg
¼ teaspoon paprika
salt and pepper
155 ml (5 fl oz/⅔ cup) single (light) cream

PAPRIKA NIBLETS: 3 slices bread
vegetable oil for frying
paprika

Discard pumpkin seeds and stringy bits.

Cut out pumpkin flesh and dice. Melt butter in a large saucepan, add onion and cook until soft. Add pumpkin, stock and sugar and bring to the boil, then cover and simmer for 30 minutes. Purée in a blender or food processor, then return to pan. Stir in nutmeg, paprika, salt and pepper and cream. Reheat gently while making the garnish.

Stamp out either attractive shapes from bread or make rings using 2 cutters, 1 slightly larger than the other. Heat enough oil to come to a depth of 0.5 cm (¼ in) in a frying pan and cook bread until golden. Drain on absorbent kitchen paper, then dust with paprika. Serve as a garnish to the soup.

Serves 6.

CONSOMMÉ MADRILÈNE

1.2 litres (2 pints/5 cups) chicken stock
500 g (1 lb) tomatoes, chopped
4 sticks celery, finely chopped
60 g (2 oz) canned pimentos, chopped
1 strip lemon peel
2 egg whites
6 teaspoons dry sherry
60 g (2 oz) pimentos, diced
1 tomato, skinned and diced
pepper

SOUP NUTS: 2 teaspoons vegetable oil
salt
1 egg
90 g (3 oz/¾ cup) plain flour
vegetable oil for frying

To make consommé, put stock, tomatoes, celery, chopped pimentos and lemon peel into a large saucepan. Whisk in egg whites and bring to the boil, stirring. Reduce heat, cover and simmer very slowly for 1 hour. To make soup nuts, put oil, ½ teaspoon salt and egg into a food processor. Add flour and mix to a smooth dough. Roll out into thin rolls about 0.5cm (¼ in) thick and leave to dry for a further 10 minutes. Snip with scissors into 0.5 cm (¼ in) pieces and leave for a further 30 minutes.

Heat oil in a deep-fat frying pan and fry soup nuts until crisp and golden. Drain on absorbent kitchen paper and use as an accompaniment to the soup. Strain consommé through a large muslin-lined sieve or colander into a bowl. Return to a clean pan and add sherry, diced pimentos and tomato. Add salt and pepper if necessary and reheat.

Serves 4-6.

— TARRAGON & TOMATO SOUP —

90 g (3 oz) bunch sorrel leaves
500 g (1 lb) ripe tomatoes
6 teaspoons olive oil
1 small onion, chopped
500 ml (16 fl oz/2 cups) vegetable stock
155 ml (5 fl oz/²⁄₃ cup) dry white wine
2 egg yolks
155 ml (5 fl oz/²⁄₃ cup) single (light) cream
salt and pepper
1 tablespoon chopped fresh tarragon
extra cream and fresh tarragon, to garnish

Trim stalks from sorrel and chop tomatoes.
Heat oil, add onion and cook until soft.

Add sorrel and tomatoes and cook for a
further 15 minutes over a very low heat. Add
stock and wine and cook for a further 10
minutes. Press the soup through a sieve into a
clean pan.

Beat egg yolks and cream together and ladle
in a little soup, then mix together. Pour back
into pan and reheat to thicken. Add salt and
pepper and stir in tarragon. Serve garnished
with a swirl of cream and a tiny sprig of
tarragon.

Serves 4-6.

— SAFFRON SOUP & QUENNELLES —

1 onion, chopped
250 g (8 oz) potatoes, chopped
250 g (8 oz) white fish fillet, skinned and chopped
940 ml (1½ pints/3¾ cups) fish stock
¼ teaspoon powdered saffron
155 ml (5 fl oz/⅔ cup) single (light) cream
salt and pepper
dill sprigs, to garnish

TROUT QUENNELLES: 250 g (8 oz) pink trout fillets,
   skinned
1 teaspoon anchovy essence
60 g (2 oz/1 cup) day-old white breadcrumbs
2 eggs, separated

Put onion, potatoes and fish in a saucepan
with fish stock, cover and gently simmer for
25 minutes, until potatoes are cooked.
Meanwhile, prepare quennelle mixture. Put
the trout into a blender or food processor with
the anchovy essence, breadcrumbs and egg
yolks and work until smooth. Turn into a
bowl and chill until the soup is ready. Blend
soup to a purée, then sieve and return to pan.
Add saffron and cream and reheat very
gently. Add salt and pepper if necessary.

Whisk egg whites until stiff and fold into the
trout mixture. Bring a pan of salted water or
fish stock to the boil, then reduce to a simmer.
Drop heaped teaspoons of trout mixture into
the water and cook for 2-3 minutes, until
they float to surface. Lift out with a slotted
spoon and place on top of the reheated soup.
Garnish with fresh dill.

Serves 6.

BOUILLABAISSE

1 kg (2 lb) mixed fish
500 g (1 lb) mixed shellfish
1 onion, sliced
1 carrot, sliced
1 stick celery, chopped
1 bay leaf
salt and pepper
6 teaspoons olive oil
2 cloves garlic, finely chopped
2 small leeks, trimmed and finely chopped
4 tomatoes, skinned and chopped
3 strips orange peel
good pinch saffron threads
1 sprig fresh thyme
slices of French bread, toasted, and Rouille, see page
    32, to serve

Clean and prepare the fish, removing the skin
and bones and cutting into chunks. Shellfish
can be left in their shells, but heads can be
removed if desired. Put fish trimmings and
bones in a large saucepan with the onion,
carrot, celery and bay leaf. Pour in 1.5 litres
(2½ pints/6 cups) water and bring to the boil.
Add salt and pepper, remove any scum which
rises to surface, cover and simmer for 30
minutes. Strain, discarding bones and
vegetables.

Heat oil in pan, add garlic and leeks and cook
over low heat for 5 minutes. Add tomatoes
and cook for 5 minutes, then pour in stock
and bring to the boil. Stir in orange peel,
saffron and thyme. When soup is boiling,
reduce heat and add white fish and simmer for
8 minutes. Add shellfish and cook for 5
minutes. Season if necessary. Serve
accompanied with French toast and rouille.

Serves 6.

— SURPRISE BEEF CONSOMMÉ —

1.2 litres (2 pints/5 cups) beef stock
250 g (8 oz) lean minced beef
1 small onion, chopped
1 carrot, chopped
2 egg whites
salt
2 teaspoons Madeira or dry sherry
1 small truffle
375 g (12 oz) puff pastry, thawed if frozen
1 egg, beaten, to glaze

To make consommé, remove any fat from stock, then put into a large heavy-based saucepan. Add meat and vegetables.

Add egg whites and slowly bring to the boil, whisking constantly. A thick grey scum will rise to the surface. Reduce heat and simmer very gently, uncovered, for 1 hour. Line a large sieve or colander with muslin and stand over a bowl. Draw back scum and ladle clarified stock into sieve or colander. The consommé should be clear and sparkling. Season with salt and Madeira or sherry. Ladle consommé into 6 individual ovenproof bowls. Cut truffle into small cubes and divide between the bowls.

Preheat oven to 200C (400F/Gas 6). Roll out pastry and cut out 6 lids to cover bowls, allowing enough to slightly overlap edges so pastry does not fall into soups. Brush tops of pastry with beaten egg, then place on a baking tray and cook in the oven for 15 minutes, until risen and golden. Serve at once.

Serves 6.

OYSTER & LEEK SOUP

18 oysters, unopened
30 g (1 oz/6 teaspoons) butter
3 leeks, trimmed and thinly sliced
1 shallot, finely chopped
125 ml (4 fl oz/½ cup) dry white wine
500 ml (16 fl oz/2 cups) light fish stock
250 ml (8 fl oz/1 cup) single (light) cream
salt and pepper
four 5 cm (2 in) rounds fried bread, to garnish

Insert point of an oyster knife or sharp, short-bladed vegetable knife at hinge of each oyster shell and twist open, holding over a bowl to catch juices. Remove each oyster and put into bowl.

Melt butter in a saucepan, add leeks and cook gently for 5 minutes, until beginning to soften. Lift out with a slotted spoon and set aside. Add shallot to pan and cook until soft. Pour in the wine and simmer for 5 minutes, uncovered. Add stock and simmer for a further 5 minutes. Meanwhile, put half the oysters in a blender or food processor with their juice and work until coarsely chopped. Cut remaining oysters in half.

Add chopped and halved oysters to soup with three-quarters of the leeks and cream and season with salt and pepper. Reheat very slowly: do not boil but maintain a heat below simmering for 3-4 minutes, until oysters are just cooked. Reheat remaining leeks in a small pan, then divide between croûtons. Float one on each portion of soup.

Serves 4.

LOBSTER BISQUE

750 g (1 1/2 lb) female lobster
90 g (3 oz/1/3 cup) butter
1 small onion, finely chopped
1 carrot, finely chopped
2 sticks celery, finely chopped
6 teaspoons brandy
155 ml (5 fl oz/2/3 cup) dry white wine
1.5 litres (2 1/2 pints/6 cups) fish stock
3 strips lemon peel
45 g (1 1/2 oz/3 tablespoons) long-grain rice
salt and pepper
2 slices toast, to garnish

Remove eggs from lobster tail and reserve.

Remove claws, and halve tail. Remove meat from body, discarding intestinal tube. Crack claws and remove meat. Discard stomach sac and gills from head part. Scoop out green 'cream' and reserve. Crush claw shells. Put softer body shell and feelers in a food processor and break up. Melt three-quarters of butter, add vegetables and cook 10 minutes. Stir in shells, pour over the brandy and ignite. When flames have subsided, add wine, three-quarters of stock and peel. Boil, then cover and simmer 25 minutes. Meanwhile, cook rice in remaining stock.

Reserve a little lobster meat, then put remainder in a food processor with the 'cream' and rice. Strain soup into a pan, add a little to the mixture in the processor and blend again. Whisk this fish mixture into the soup, season and gently reheat. Cut out 6 small rounds from the toast. Heat remaining butter in a small pan, add reserved fish eggs and cook to warm them through. Spoon on to toast for garnish and any remaining can be stirred into soup with reserved lobster.

Serves 6.

— CREAM OF BROCCOLI SOUP —

30 g (1 oz/6 teaspoons) butter
2 shallots, finely chopped
500 g (1 lb) broccoli flowerets, chopped
1 large potato, diced
1 clove garlic, crushed
500 ml (16 fl oz/2 cups) vegetable stock
500 ml (16 fl oz/2 cups) milk
salt and pepper
pinch grated nutmeg

TO GARNISH: 155 ml (5 fl oz/²⁄₃ cup) single (light) cream
15 g (½ oz/2 tablespoons) ground almonds
¼ teaspoon powdered saffron

Melt butter in a large saucepan, add shallots
and cook for 2-3 minutes, until soft. Add
broccoli, potato and garlic, cover and cook
gently for 5 minutes. Add stock and bring to
the boil, then cover and simmer for 20
minutes, until vegetables are tender. Purée in
a blender or food processor, then return soup
to pan and add milk and salt and pepper and
nutmeg. Reheat gently.

To garnish, divide cream between 2 bowls.
Mix ground almonds into one and saffron
into the other. Ladle soup into individual
bowls and place alternate swirls of cream
mixtures on top of each.

Serves 4.

— THAI CUCUMBER & PORK SOUP —

4 Chinese dried mushrooms, soaked for 20 minutes in
   hot water and drained
940 ml (1½ pints/3¾ cups) chicken stock
3 teaspoons cornflour
185 g (6 oz) pork tenderloin, cut into thin strips
6 teaspoons soy sauce
6 teaspoons rice vinegar
½ cucumber, cut into thin strips
185 g (6 oz) Chinese leaves, finely shredded

Remove stalks from mushrooms and cut into
thin slices, then put into a saucepan with
stock, and bring to the boil.

On a large plate, sprinkle cornflour over pork
strips and roll lightly to coat. Add to stock
with soy sauce and vinegar and simmer for 5
minutes.

Stir in cucumber and Chinese leaves and
simmer for a further 2 minutes: do not
overcook otherwise texture and flavour will
be lost. Transfer to serving bowls.

Serves 4-6.

— RED & YELLOW PEPPER SOUP —

60 g (2 oz/¼ cup) butter
1 large onion, chopped
2 cloves garlic, crushed
250 g (8 oz) tomatoes, coarsely chopped
250 g (8 oz) red peppers and 250 g (8 oz) yellow
    peppers (capsicums), seeded and chopped
1.2 litres (2 pints/5 cups) vegetable stock
salt and pepper
3 teaspoons arrowroot
30 g (1 oz) blanched almonds or pine nuts
30 g (1 oz) white bread, crusts removed
125 ml (4 fl oz/½ cup) single (light) cream

Put half the butter, half the onion and 1 clove
garlic in a saucepan.

Put remaining butter, onion and garlic in
another pan. Cook both gently until onion
has softened. In one pan, add tomatoes, red
peppers (capsicums) and half the stock. Add
yellow peppers (capsicums) and remaining
stock to the other pan. Cover both pans and
simmer for 20 minutes. Purée, then sieve
each soup separately and return to separate
pans. Add salt and pepper. Blend arrowroot
with a little water and stir into red pepper
(capsicum) soup and reheat to thicken.

Put almonds or pine nuts, bread and cream
into a blender or food processor and purée.
Stir this mixture into yellow pepper
(capsicum) soup and reheat. To serve, pour
each soup into a jug, and pour into individual
bowls, pouring red pepper (capsicum) soup
from one side and yellow pepper (capsicum)
soup from the opposite side. Serve at once.

Serves 6.

WATERCRESS CONSOMMÉ

940 ml (1½ pints/3¾ cups) Beef Consommé, see page 108
2 small carrots, cannelled and sliced (see Note)
12 sprigs fresh watercress
9 teaspoons Madeira
salt and pepper

HERBY PASTA: 125 g (4 oz/1 cup) plain flour
1 egg, beaten
1 teaspoon vegetable oil
2 teaspoons finely chopped fresh herbs

To make pasta, put flour into a bowl. Make a well in centre and add egg, oil, herbs and 9 teaspoons water.

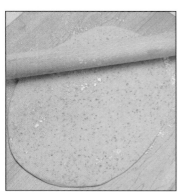

Mix into the flour until the dough is soft and pliable. Turn onto a floured surface and knead until smooth. Wrap dough and leave to rest for 30 minutes. Roll dough out thinly, cover with a cloth and leave to dry for 30 minutes, turning over after 15 minutes. Meanwhile, put consommé in a saucepan with carrots and stalks from watercress and simmer for 8 minutes.

Bring a pan of salted water to the boil. Cut out small fancy shapes from pasta, then drop into boiling water and cook for about 8 minutes, until tender. Remove watercress stalks from soup, stir in the Madeira, watercress leaves and salt and pepper. Drain pasta, add to consommé and serve hot.

Serves 4-6.

Note: Use a cannelle knife to remove strips of peel down length of each carrot to give a decorative pattern when sliced.

ORIENTAL SCALLOP SOUP

8 scallops
2 teaspoons chopped fresh root ginger
6 teaspoons dry sherry
3 teaspoons light soy sauce
940 ml (1½ pints/3¾ cups) chicken stock
2 cloves garlic, thinly sliced
½ red pepper (capsicum), cut into diamonds
½ yellow pepper (capsicum), cut into diamonds
60 g (2 oz) pea starch noodles, soaked for 5 minutes,
   then drained
salt and pepper

Rinse scallops and drain. Quarter white parts and put in a bowl with ginger, sherry and soy sauce.

Stir to coat scallops with marinade, then set aside. Reserve pink corals. Pour stock into a large saucepan, add garlic and bring to the boil. Cover and simmer for 15 minutes. Add peppers (capsicums) and noodles and cook for 3 minutes, until noodles are tender.

Stir in scallops with marinade and corals and cook for about 2 minutes, until white parts turn opaque. Add salt and pepper and serve at once.

Serves 4.

— SMOKED SALMON & DILL SOUP —

30 g (1 oz/6 teaspoons) butter
2 shallots, finely chopped
15 g (½ oz/6 teaspoons) plain flour
625 ml (20 fl oz/2½ cups) milk
½ fish stock cube
1 cucumber, peeled and chopped
185 g (6 oz) smoked salmon bits
1 tablespoon chopped fresh dill
155 ml (5 fl oz/⅔ cup) single (light) cream
salt and pepper

Melt butter in a pan, add shallots and cook until soft. Stir in flour and cook for 1 minute, then gradually stir in milk. Bring to boil and crumble in stock cube, then add cucumber.

Simmer stock for 10 minutes. Reserve a few of better bits of salmon for garnish, then chop remainder and add to soup and cook for 2-3 minutes.

Purée in a blender or food processor until smooth. Return to pan, add dill and cream and salt and pepper if necessary and gently reheat. Serve garnished with small pieces of reserved smoked salmon.

Serves 4.

— CREAM OF ASPARAGUS SOUP —

750 g (1½ lb) thin asparagus spears
45 g (1½ oz/9 teaspoons) butter
1 bunch spring onions, chopped
15 g (½ oz/6 teaspoons) plain flour
940 ml (1½ pints/3¾ cups) light chicken stock
2 egg yolks
155 ml (5 fl oz/⅔ cup) single (light) cream
salt and pepper
single (light) cream, to garnish

Wash asparagus, cut off tips and gently simmer in salted water for 3-5 minutes, until just tender. Drain and set aside. Cut off woody ends, scrape stalks to remove scales and then chop.

Melt butter in a saucepan, add chopped asparagus and spring onions and cook together for 5 minutes. Stir in flour and cook for 1 minute, then gradually add stock. Simmer for 20-25 minutes, until asparagus is tender.

Cool soup slightly, then purée in a blender or food processor and sieve back into pan. Beat egg yolks in a bowl, then whisk in a little soup, and return to pan. Add cream and reheat gently until soup has a creamy texture, stirring. Add salt and pepper. Stir in reserved asparagus tips and heat for 2 minutes. Serve each portion with a swirl of cream.

Serves 6.

GAZPACHO

500 g (1 lb) ripe tomatoes, skinned and chopped
½ cucumber, peeled and chopped
1 green pepper (capsicum), seeded and chopped
1 red pepper (capsicum), seeded and chopped
1 small onion, chopped
1 clove garlic, chopped
60 g (2 oz/1 cup) soft breadcrumbs
6 teaspoons olive oil
6 teaspoons red wine vinegar
500 ml (16 fl oz/2 cups) tomato juice
½ teaspoon dried marjoram
salt and pepper

Put all soup ingredients into a blender or food processor, in 2 batches if necessary.

Blend until smooth. The soup should be the consistency of single (light) cream; if it is too thick add a little iced water. Turn the soup into a bowl, cover and refrigerate for about 2 hours before serving.

When the soup is well chilled, season if necessary and add few ice cubes.

Serves 4-6.

Note: Gazpacho is traditionally served with a selection of garnishes handed round separately to be added to individual portions as desired. Put 2 chopped hard-boiled eggs, finely diced ½ cucumber, finely chopped onion, 12 stoned and chopped green or black olives and 1 diced green pepper (capsicum) into separate small bowls.